Margaret Evelyn Jordan Buttram
July 3, 1911-April 27, 1990

Pam's Healthy Southern Kitchen

Old Fashioned Southern Recipes
From Momma Buttram's Kitchen

Pamela Hudson

Printed in the United States of America

First Printing, 2014

ISBN-13: 978-0692289334

Published by P & B Arts, LLC

www.pamshealthysouthernkitchen.com

Cover Photograph by Samantha Taylor

In Loving Memory of Margaret Evelyn Jordan Buttram

Special thanks to my husband, Billy for his support and being a great taste tester and to my sister, Margaret for helping me to remember how 'Momma did it'.

A wife of noble character who can find? She is worth far more than rubies. Her husband has full confidence in her and lacks nothing of value. She brings him good, not harm, all the days of her life. She selects wool and flax and works with eager hands. She is like the merchant ships, bringing her food from afar. She gets up while it is still night; she provides food for her family and portions for her female servants. She considers a field and buys it; out of her earnings she plants a vineyard. She sets about her work vigorously; her arms are strong for her tasks. She sees that her trading is profitable, and her lamp does not go out at night. In her hand she holds the distaff and grasps the spindle with her fingers. She opens her arms to the poor and extends her hands to the needy. When it snows, she has no fear for her household; for all of them are clothed in scarlet. She makes coverings for her bed; she is clothed in fine linen and purple. Her husband is respected at the city gate, where he takes his seat among the elders of the land. She makes linen garments and sells them, and supplies the merchants with sashes. She is clothed with strength and dignity; she can laugh at the days to come. She speaks with wisdom, and faithful instruction is on her tongue. She watches over the affairs of her household and does not eat the bread of idleness. Her children arise and call her blessed; her husband also, and he praises her: "Many women do noble things, but you surpass them all." Charm is deceptive, and beauty is fleeting; but a woman who fears the LORD is to be praised. Honor her for all that her hands have done, and let her works bring her praise at the city gate. Proverbs 31, verses 10-31 New International Version Bible

My Momma, Margaret Evelyn Jordan Buttram was nicknamed Momma Buttram by my best friend and her Mama. I was born when she was 43 years old so my girlfriends had Grandmothers who were around her age. Momma Buttram was born in 1911 in Cedartown, GA. Cedartown was a mill town, you farmed or you worked in one of the mills. Momma and Daddy tried both. Daddy loved to farm but Momma loved town so they spent most of their early married years raising children and working in the mill. They did their share of picking cotton and Momma talked about that until she died. I guess if you ever had to be out in the hot sun picking cotton all day with a bag slung over your shoulder that got heavier the more you picked you never forgot it. She lived through World War I, the Great Depression and World War II. Her cooking and lifestyle for the rest of her life were affected by these events. They lived in the mill village with other mill workers. She told me that she and her friends in the village would share a piece of fatback to cook in their dried beans. Their prize possession was a Milk Cow, everyone had them back then. Momma Buttram's recipes were simple but very tasty. She didn't use a lot of spices or herbs and her food seasoned with salt and pepper was just delicious. Her biscuits were very unusual. They were not flakey, they were more like loaf bread. The biscuits didn't break up so you could cut them open and put anything in them and it was like eating a small sandwich. She made biscuits twice a day. She would get up at 5:30 each morning and cook biscuits for breakfast and Daddy would take biscuits for lunch. If it was after payday, he would have sausage or ham biscuits, closer to payday, he would have cheese or butter and jelly. Most nights we had cornbread AND biscuits. Daddy expected biscuits at supper and then he would usually eat cornbread and buttermilk before going to bed. Momma used lard in her biscuits until Daddy had his heart attack at 62, he stopped smoking and she stopped using lard. That gave him 13 more years of life. Momma's family was from Ireland so we ate a lot of potatoes. To this day, give me some dried beans, potatoes, cole slaw and corn bread and I am a happy girl. Dried beans, we had them every weekday. She put them into soak in the morning and started cooking them around 2pm.

Daddy's dream was to make a living farming. That never happened. Momma hated the country and my brothers had different dreams. What my Daddy left to me was a love of growing things. Even after he got a job at the railroad and moved to the big city, he always had a garden and grew plums, pears, blueberries and figs in his yard. He raised chickens for eggs and we traveled deep into the country outside of Cedartown to buy fresh butter. Daddy always said that if people grew their own food it would solve lots of problems.

I haven't always been a vegetarian but I always preferred vegetables over meat. I have a friend who is a diabetic, two friends who have celiac disease, a friend who stays on a low carb diet most of the time, another friend who gets sick if she doesn't have a meat protein at each meal. My husband is a meat eater but he also benefits from all of the fruits and vegetables that I prepare. Everyone is different and I believe we have to find the way that works best for us. I cook meat for my husband and friends and I make an effort to serve food that everyone who comes to my house can eat. Eating a healthy diet can be as simple as eating no fast food and preparing as many meals as you can at home from fresh ingredients.

I grind wheat and grains for my bread and baked goods and I recognize that most people don't due to time or money constraints. When I wrote my first cookbook "Pam's Healthy Southern Kitchen, Baking with Freshly Milled Flour, No Eggs,

No Butter", my brother and sister in law who are in their 80's and 70's respectively decided they wanted to bake bread, muffins, pies and cookies from the book. They bought a Kitchen Aid Mixer and Whole Grain Flour and started baking. I was so proud of them. To me, this is what healthy eating is: Doing your best to cook wholesome food at home using the most natural ingredients you can find.

This cookbook is a mixture of my Momma's recipes and my own. I took a few of her recipes and made them Vegan and some recipes are from my dear friends and family.

MENUS

Momma Buttram had her own menus so if you knew which dried bean was soaking, you knew the rest of the meal. She had her menus for Weekdays, Sunday or Company and Christmas. If it was during the summer and Daddy's garden was 'coming in' the menus would include fresh green beans, tomatoes, green onions, squash, hot and banana peppers or anything that was ready for pickin'. If she had the fixings she would throw in a salad, cole slaw or can of whole tomatoes. She also made great homemade chili and soup. My favorite summer lunch was sautéed green onions picked out of the yard and pan fried cornbread.

THE WEEKDAY MENUS

Dried Black-Eyed Peas
Kraut and Wieners
Fried Irish Potatoes
Biscuits

Dried Large Lima Beans
Cheese and Macaroni
Creamed Beef
Biscuits and Corn Bread

Dried Baby Lima Beans
Goulash
Candied Sweet Potatoes
Biscuits and Corn Bread

Dried Pinto Beans
Hominy
Meatloaf
Biscuits

Dried Large Lima Beans
Meat Balls and Potatoes
Biscuits and Cornbread

Barbecued Chicken
Baked Beans
Mashed Potatoes or Potatoes In White Sauce
Cole Slaw
Biscuits

Fried Salmon Patties
Creamed Corn
Mashed Potatoes
English Peas
Biscuits

SATURDAY NIGHT MENU
Fried Oysters
Oyster Stew
Green Olives
Ketchup
Biscuits

THE SUNDAY MENUS

Fried Chicken
Cream Gravy
Mashed Potatoes
English Peas
Baked Beans
Biscuits

Beef Roast or Pork Roast with Sweet Potatoes or Ham
Green Beans
Potato Salad
Deviled Eggs
Biscuits and Cornbread

CHRISTMAS MENU

Chicken and Dressing
Giblet Gravy
Cranberry Sauce
Green Beans
Potato Salad
Deviled Eggs
Butter Peas
Macaroni and Cheese
Cole Slaw

The Christmas Desserts were as important as the meal.

Lane Cake
Raisin Cake
Japanese Fruit Cake
Old Fashioned Dark Fruitcake
Ambrosia
Divinity Candy
Chocolate Fudge
Date Nut Roll
Orange Slices Candy
Vanilla Cream Dark Chocolate Drops
Chocolate Covered Cherries Candy
Salted Nuts

Meats and Main Dishes

Barbecue Chicken

I remember eating this Barbecue Chicken, the meat was so tender.

1 Whole Chicken cut up in pieces
1 - 12oz can Coca Cola
1 cup Ketchup

1. Mix Coca Cola and Ketchup together.
2. Pour mixture over Chicken in an electric skillet.
3. Start cooking on 400 for five minutes then on 275 until tender and sauce is thick. Cook about 2 hours, uncover last ½ hour.

*If you don't have an electric skillet, cook on the stove on medium high until mixture starts to cook then turn down to low. I use a 15 inch cast iron skillet with a lid.

Beef Roast with Potatoes, Carrots and Onions

A typical "Sunday Dinner" at Momma Buttram's House.

2 1/2 to 3 pound Chuck Roast
4 medium Potatoes cut in fourths
5 medium Carrots cut in 2 inch pieces
4 small Onions cut in half or 2 medium cut in fourths
2 1/2 teaspoons Salt divided
2 1/2 teaspoons Pepper divided
5 Garlic Cloves peeled (Optional)

1. Preheat Oven to 350 degrees.
2. Spray a large Casserole Dish with Lid with Cooking Spray or use Heavy Duty Aluminum Foil, a large enough piece to cover Roast and Vegetables.
3. Place Chuck Roast in Dish or on aluminum foil.
4. Sprinkle 1 teaspoons Salt and Pepper on each side of Roast.
5. Place Potatoes, Carrots and Onions (and Garlic if using) around Roast and sprinkle 1/2 teaspoon Salt and Pepper over Vegetables.
6. Cover Roast and Potatoes and cook 2 to 2 1/2 hours.
7. If roast isn't tender after 2 1/2 hours, take vegetables out and set aside and let roast cook another 30 minutes.

*If Momma didn't have the potatoes, carrots and onions, she would use sweet potatoes instead.

Beef Roast with Onion Gravy

Billy's Daddy was a great cook. You could smell his Sunday Dinner as soon as you got out of your car. Here is his version of a Beef Roast.

2 1/2 to 3 pound Chuck Roast
4 tablespoons Vegetable Oil
½ cup Self-Rising Flour
1 teaspoon Salt
1 teaspoon Pepper
2 Onions sliced
4 chopped Garlic Cloves
2 cups Water

1. Heat Oil in a pan large enough for the Roast to lay flat in the pan. I used a 10 inch Enamel Cast Iron pan with lid.
2. Sprinkle Salt and Pepper over both sides of Roast and dredge in Flour coating Roast completely.
3. Over medium high heat, let Roast brown on both sides, about 4 to 5 minutes each side.
4. Place sliced Onions and Garlic in pan and add 2 cups of water.
5. Cover, reduce heat to medium low and let Roast, Onions and Garlic cook for 2 hours.
6. The last 30 minutes of cooking, remove the lid so the gravy with thicken up.

Beef Stew

1 pound package of Stew Beef
1/4 cup All Purpose Flour
1/2 teaspoon Salt
1/2 teaspoon Pepper
2 tablespoons Vegetable Oil
1 medium Onion cut in chunks
2 Garlic Cloves minced
2 stalks Celery chopped
14.5 ounce can Italian Diced Tomatoes with Herbs
2 cans Water (this rinses out the herbs and tomatoes
    from the can so you don't waste anything)
1 teaspoon Salt
1/2 teaspoon Pepper
1 large Potato peeled and cut in large pieces
2 Carrots cut in 2 inch pieces
1/2 cup frozen Green Peas

1. Sprinkle 1/2 teaspoon Salt and 1/2 teaspoon Pepper over Stew Beef and dredge in Flour.
2. Brown Stew Beef in hot Vegetable Oil in a large pan with lid.
3. Add Onion, Garlic, Celery, Tomatoes, Water, 1 teaspoon Salt and 1/2 teaspoon Pepper.
4. Cover and simmer 1 hour.
5. Add Potatoes and Carrots and cook about 15-20 minutes until Potatoes and Carrots are tender.
6. Add 1/2 cup frozen Peas and cook 2 minutes.

Chicken Casserole

Momma liked to make this for Church Socials.

1 Whole Chicken (or use All Chicken Breasts)
2 cans Cream of Chicken Soup
8 ounce carton Sour Cream
1 roll Ritz Crackers
1 stick melted Butter or Margarine
Poppy Seeds (optional)

1. Preheat oven to 350 degrees.
2. Boil Chicken, when tender and done let Chicken cool and remove skin and bones, cut up Chicken and spread in a greased baking dish.
3. Mix Cream of Chicken Soup and Sour Cream together. Pour over chicken and spread evenly.
4. Crush Ritz crackers and sprinkle over mixture.
5. Melt Butter or Margarine and pour over crackers.
6. If using Poppy Seeds, sprinkle over the top.
7. Bake 15 to 20 minutes.

Chicken Stuffing Casserole

Momma Buttram was a character and one of the stories that still makes me laugh happened on a Sunday morning at the local Independent Baptist Church. Momma was hard of hearing so she talked loud. One of the long winded Deacons was praying and people were getting tired of standing and they were silently praying he would come to the end. The Deacon started winding down and said, "Lord, I believe I could pray all day". Momma Buttram was heard in the silence saying, "Lord, I believe he's going to".

1 Whole Chicken
1 can Peas and Carrots
1 can Cream of Chicken Soup
1 can Cream of Celery Soup
1 package Pepperidge Farm Cornbread Stuffing Mix
3 cups Chicken Broth

1. Preheat Oven to 350 degrees.
2. Boil Chicken until done and tender about 1 hour. Remove all bones and skin and chop Chicken and place in the bottom of a greased casserole dish. Set Broth aside.
3. Drain Peas and Carrots and place on top of the Chicken.
4. Mix Cream of Chicken Soup and Cream of Celery Soup together and spoon over Chicken and Peas and Carrots.
5. Sprinkle package of Cornbread Stuffing Mix over the top.
6. Pour 3 cups Chicken Broth over stuffing until completely saturated.
7. Bake for about 1 hour.

Chicken and Dressing

Momma never bought a Turkey, she always bought a hen and boiled it to get her broth for the dressing.

1 Hen
Salt and Pepper to taste (about 1 teaspoon Salt and 1/2 teaspoon Pepper)

1. Save Giblets Packet for your Giblet Gravy.
2. Boil Hen in water seasoned with Salt and Pepper until done about 1 hour.
3. Cut up Hen and save Broth for dressing.

Dressing

2 tablespoon Canola Oil
1 small Onion chopped
1/2 cup Celery chopped
6 Momma Buttram's Homemade Biscuits (Pages 71, 72)
1/2 pone of Momma Buttram's Cornbread (Page 73)
10 slices of White Loaf Bread
1/2 cup Butter
1 tablespoon Sage
1/2 teaspoon Salt
1/2 teaspoon Pepper
2 eggs beaten
4 cups Chicken Broth   (you can use canned if you want to roast your Hen or Turkey)

1. Preheat Oven to 350 degrees.
2. Grease an oblong 9x13 inch Pan.
3. Sauté Onion and Celery in Oil. Set aside to cool.
4. Break up Biscuits, Cornbread and Loaf Bread in large bowl.
5. Pour warm Broth over bread to soak.
6. Add Chopped Onion and Celery that have been sautéed in Oil.
7. Melt Butter and add to mixture.

8. Add Sage (Momma used lots of ground sage), Salt and Pepper to taste. If you need more sage add it, sage makes the dressing good. Go easy on the salt as your broth may have added salt. I always taste before I add the eggs. If you need more broth add enough so that the dressing is not dry. The mixture should be wet but not soupy.

9. Add Eggs and stir until well mixed.

10. Pour into a greased pan and bake at 350 about 30 minutes until done (it should be light brown and firm).

*To make vegetarian, use Vegetable Broth instead of Chicken Broth.

Giblet Gravy

Giblets
2 tablespoons Butter
3 tablespoons Flour
1/4 teaspoon Salt
1/8 teaspoon Pepper
2 cups liquid from boiling Giblets
1 boiled Egg chopped

1. Place Giblets in a small pan and cover with water. Boil until done about 40 minutes.

2. Cut up Liver and Gizzard and reserve Broth.

3. Melt Butter in a pan and add Flour, 1/4 teaspoon Salt and 1/8 teaspoon Pepper. Cook and stir two minutes.

4. Add Broth and cook until thick. Stir in Giblets and Chopped Boiled Egg. Serve over Dressing or Chicken.

Chicken and Dumplings

3 to 4 pound Chicken
3 quarts of Water
1 teaspoon Salt
1/4 teaspoon Pepper
1 Recipe of Momma Buttram's Biscuit Dough (Pages 71, 72)

1. Place Chicken in a large stock pot and add water. Add Salt and Pepper.
2. Bring Chicken and Water to a Boil. Reduce heat, cover and cook for 1 to 1 1/2 hours or until Chicken is done and very tender.
3. Remove Chicken, let cool and cut up in pieces removing skin and bones.
4. Skim the fat off the top of the broth. Taste broth and add more Salt and Pepper if needed. You will probably need 1 teaspoon Salt and 1/2 teaspoon Pepper.
5. Roll biscuit dough out on a floured board about 1/4 of an inch. Cut dough into 1 inch by 4 inch pieces.
6. Drop dough pieces one at a time into boiling broth. Let this mixture cook gently for 10 minutes stirring occasionally to keep dough from sticking to the bottom of the pan.
7. Place Chicken back into broth and simmer to heat the chicken.

*If you prefer, you can use canned biscuits.

Chicken Brunswick Stew

This stew was one of Momma's specialties. This recipe requires a slow cooker.

1 Whole Chicken
2 medium Potatoes diced
1 medium Onion diced
No. 2 can Tomatoes (20 ounce Can)
½ cup Barbecue Sauce
½ cup Ketchup
dash Worcestershire Sauce
No. 2 can Cream Style Corn (20 ounce Can)
Salt and Pepper to taste

1. Before going to bed at night put Whole Chicken, Potatoes, Onions and Tomatoes into slow cooker.
2. Cook all night on low.
3. In the morning remove Chicken from pot, skin and remove bones. Return meat to pot and add Ketchup, Barbecue Sauce and Worcestershire Sauce.
4. Cook all day on low or until ready to eat. Add Corn, Salt and Pepper and cook a few minutes longer.

Fried Chicken with Cream Gravy

A typical Sunday Dinner in the South.

1 Chicken (2 breasts, 2 thighs, 2 wings and 2 drumsticks)
1/2 cup Self-Rising Flour or more if needed
Salt and Pepper to Taste
Vegetable Oil

1. Season Chicken with Salt and Pepper. (Sprinkle both sides with Salt and Pepper from shaker.)
2. Place Flour in a pie plate.
3. Place Vegetable Oil in a cast iron skillet until skillet is a little less than half full.
4. Heat Vegetable Oil to 350 degrees.
5. Dredge Chicken in Flour and place in hot oil.
6. Cook Chicken about 15 minutes for dark meet and 10 minutes for white meat, turning occasionally and make sure chicken is brown on all sides.

*Use a Meat Thermometer to make sure your Chicken is done. 165 degrees or until juices run clear.

Chicken Gravy

4 tablespoons Oil that you fried the Chicken in
4 tablespoons Flour
2 cups Milk
1/2 teaspoon Salt
1/4 teaspoon Pepper

1. Heat Oil in skillet.
2. Add Flour and stir until mixture starts to turn brown (about 1 - 2 minutes). Add Salt and Pepper.
3. Stir in Milk and let gravy cook about 10 minutes until thick.

Pam's Oven Fried Chicken and Cream Gravy

My husband said this is the best chicken he has ever had. Cooking it in the oven makes it very tender.

1 Chicken (2 breasts, 2 thighs, 2 wings and 2 drumsticks)
1/2 cup of Self-Rising Flour or more if needed
Salt and Pepper to Taste
Paprika
1/4 to 1/2 cup Vegetable Oil depending on size of pan

1. Preheat Oven to 425.
2. Season Chicken with Salt, Pepper and Paprika on both sides. (Sprinkle both sides with Salt, Pepper and Paprika from shaker.)
3. Place Flour in a pie plate.
4. Place Vegetable Oil in a large oven proof pan that will hold all the chicken. Place enough oil in pan to just cover the bottom of pan. You may have to use two pans depending on the size of your chicken pieces.
5. Place pan in oven to heat the oil while you prepare the chicken. If you are using cast iron, you can heat oil on top of the stove.
6. Dredge Chicken in flour and place in the pan with hot oil.
7. Bake 30 minutes, then turn chicken and bake 15 minutes longer.

Gravy

4 tablespoons Vegetable Oil
4 tablespoons Flour
2 cups Milk
1/2 teaspoon Salt
1/4 teaspoon Pepper

1. Heat Oil in skillet.
2. Add Flour and stir until mixture starts to turn brown (about 1 - 2 minutes). Add Salt and Pepper.
3. Stir in Milk and let gravy cook about 10 minutes until thick.
*To make Vegan Gravy, use Soy Milk.

Spanish Chicken

1 Hen
1 box Yellow Rice
1 can Green Peas drained
1 can Tomatoes broken up or mashed
1 can Cream of Celery Soup
1 small Onion Chopped

1. Boil Hen until tender about 1 hour and take meat off the bone. Save the broth.
2. Preheat oven to 350 degrees.
3. Place Rice, Peas, Tomatoes, Cream of Celery Soup and Onion in a large baking dish and mix together.
4. Place Chicken on top of mixture and cover with Broth and add some hot water if needed.
5. Cover with foil or lid and bake for 1 1/2 hours.

Country Fried Steak and Gravy

4 Cube Steaks
1/2 cup Self-Rising Flour
1 teaspoon Salt
1/2 teaspoon Pepper
1/4 cup Vegetable Oil

1. Place Flour, Salt and Pepper on a plate and mix together until combined.
2. Place Oil in a non-stick skillet or a cast iron skillet. Heat over medium high heat while preparing Steaks.
3. Dredge Cubed Steaks in Flour mixture one at a time.
4. Place Steaks in hot Oil and let cook 8 to 10 minutes each side turning occasionally after Steaks have browned. Cook until Steaks are done which will be 15 to 20 minutes.

Gravy

2 tablespoons Vegetable Oil
4 tablespoons Self-Rising Flour
1/2 teaspoon Salt
1/4 teaspoon Pepper
2 cups Milk

1. Using skillet with oil that you cooked the Steaks in, add 2 tablespoons more Vegetable Oil.
2. Stir in Flour, Salt and Pepper and let cook 3 to 4 minutes.
3. Add Milk and stir until smooth.
4. Let gravy cook 10 minutes until thick and bubbly.

Creamed Beef

This is a really quick and easy dish. Momma usually had Dried Baby Lima Beans with Creamed Beef.

1 tablespoon Vegetable Oil
2 tablespoons Self-Rising Flour
1/4 teaspoon Salt
1/8 teaspoon Pepper
1 cup Milk
12 ounce can Roast Beef with Gravy

1. In a non-stick skillet, heat Vegetable Oil over medium heat.
2. Add Flour, stir and cook 1 minute.
3. Add Salt and Pepper.
4. Stir in Milk, turn heat down to medium low and let mixture cook 5 minutes stirring often. The mixture will not be very thick at this time.
5. Add the can of Roast Beef and Gravy. Stir and break up Beef with the back of a wooden spoon.
6. Increase heat to medium and let mixture come to a boil stirring constantly. The desired thickness should be reached in 8 to 10 minutes.

Creole Burgers

This recipe is similar to Momma's Scrambled Burger.

1 pound Ground Beef or Chuck
2 tablespoons Vegetable Oil
1/2 minced Onion
1/3 chopped Green Pepper
1 can Condensed Tomato Soup
1/4 cup Water
1 teaspoon Salt
1 teaspoon Chili Powder
1/2 teaspoon Thyme
1 tablespoon Vinegar
6 slices Cheese
6 Hamburger Buns

1. Brown Meat in Oil and add Onions and Green Peppers. Cook about 5 minutes longer.
2. Add Tomato Soup, Water, Salt, Chili Powder, Thyme and Vinegar and simmer over low heat uncovered for about 30 minutes or until thick.
3. Cut bun in half and place a slice of cheese on bottom half of each bun.
4. Arrange buns on broiler pan and toast.
5. Place generous spoonful of meat mixture on top of melted cheese and cover with other half of bun.

Momma Buttram's Famous Scrambled Burgers

I remember eating these for lunch with Momma when I was out of school for the summer. I found a handwritten recipe for a Creole Burger that Momma had saved. It is similar to her Scrambled Burger but has more ingredients and spices.

1/2 pound Ground Chuck
1/2 teaspoon Salt
1/4 teaspoon Pepper
Mustard
Ketchup
Dill Pickle Slices
Chopped Onion
White Loaf Bread

1. Cook Ground Chuck in skillet and separate with wooden spoon like you are cooking meat for spaghetti. Salt and Pepper to taste.
2. When meat is done drain on paper towels.
3. Put ketchup and mustard on bread and top with meat.
4. Add Onion and Dill Pickles if desired.

Lasagna

Momma never made Lasagna, I started making it when I was in high school and she loved it. This is great to make when you have a crowd coming over. Put it together a day or two ahead and place in the refrigerator and then bake it on the day of your party.

1 pound Ground Chuck
24 ounce jar Spaghetti Sauce
1 cup Water
4 cups Grated Mozzarella Cheese
15 ounce container Cottage Cheese
½ cup Grated Parmesan Cheese
16 Lasagna Noodles, cooked

1. Preheat oven to 350 degrees.
2. Cook Lasagna Noodles according to package directions or use no cook Lasagna Noodles.
3. Brown meat in skillet on medium high heat. When meat is done, remove meat and drain grease from pan.
4. Place cooked meat, Spaghetti Sauce and 1 cup Water in pan and simmer 10 minutes.
5. Spread 1 cup of meat sauce on the bottom of a greased 13x9 inch baking dish.
6. Top with a layer of 4 Lasagna Noodles.
7. Place 1/4 of Meat Sauce, 1/3 of the Cottage Cheese and 1 cup of the Mozzarella Cheese over the Noodles.
8. Repeat this layer twice.
9. Top with remaining Lasagna Noodles, Meat Sauce, Mozzarella and Parmesan Cheese.
10. Cover with aluminum foil sprayed with cooking spray so cheese won't stick.
11. Bake 1 hour and remove foil after 45 minutes. Let stand 15 minutes before serving.

Baked Ham

This is Billy's recipe for baked ham. Everyone loves this especially at our Christmas Parties.

Fully Cooked Butt Portion Ham
1 can Coca Cola

1. Preheat oven to 350 degrees.
2. Place Ham in a large oven proof pan lined with enough aluminum foil to cover ham or place in a large pan with lid.
3. Pour the can of Coca Cola over the ham.
4. Bake 1 hour and 30 minutes.

Ham Soup

1/4 cup (1/2 stick) Butter
1/4 cup Onion chopped
2 cups diced raw Potatoes
1/4 cup Water
1/4 cup All Purpose Flour
1/2 teaspoon Salt
1/4 teaspoon Marjoram
1/8 teaspoon Pepper
1/8 teaspoon Celery Salt
3 cups Milk
10 ounce package Frozen Peas thawed
1 1/2 cups (1/2 pound) diced cooked Ham
Wedge of Blue Cheese (optional)

1. Melt Butter in heavy 2 quart saucepan with lid.
2. Add Onion, Potatoes and Water. Bring to a boil. Lower heat to simmer and cook until potatoes are tender about 15 minutes. Stir and add more water if needed so potatoes don't stick to the pan.
3. Stir in Flour, Salt, Marjoram, Pepper, and Celery Salt.
4. Add Milk slowly and cook until thickened stirring constantly.
5. Stir in Peas and Ham and simmer 5 minutes or until Peas are cooked.
6. Serve with a wedge of crumbled Blue Cheese over soup if desired.

Goulash

Momma always had Baby Lima Beans or Large Lima Beans with Goulash.

1 cup Dried Macaroni Noodles cooked according to package directions
1 pound Ground Chuck
1/2 teaspoon Salt
1/4 teaspoon Black Pepper
1 cup chopped Onion
1/2 cup chopped Green Bell Pepper
15 ounce can Tomato Sauce

1. Cook Macaroni Noodles according to package directions.
2. While Macaroni is cooking, place Ground Chuck in a skillet, break up and cook on medium high heat. Sprinkle Salt and Pepper over meat.
3. When meat is starting to brown and giving off liquid, add Onion and Bell Pepper and let cook with meat until they start to soften.
4. Stir in Tomato Sauce and cooked Macaroni and let simmer on low 10 minutes.

*You can use Ground Turkey or to make it Vegan, you can use a little oil and brown some Vegan Boca Crumbles or any Vegan Ground Meat Substitute.

Kraut and Wieners

Momma always served these with Black Eyed Peas, Fried Irish Potatoes and Biscuits. This is still one of my favorite meals. I use Vegan Hot Dogs instead of All Beef Wieners.

2 teaspoons Oil
6 All Beef Wieners
14 ounce can Sauerkraut

1. Heat Oil in non-stick pan.
2. Cut Wieners in 1/2 inch rounds and sauté in hot oil.
3. When Wieners are cooked, add Sauerkraut and heat thoroughly.

Meatballs and Potatoes

This very simple recipe was one of Momma's staples. No one loved this better than my niece, Rebecca.

1 pound Ground Chuck
4 cups Potatoes cut in pieces about the same size as the
    Meatballs
1 small Onion, diced
¾ cups Water
15 ounce can Tomato Sauce
1 teaspoon Salt
½ teaspoon Pepper

1. Make Meatballs out of Ground Chuck, you should have about 8 Meatballs. Place on a plate and set aside.
2. Peel and cut Potatoes into pieces about the same size as the Meatballs. Place Potatoes in a large saucepan.
3. Peel and dice Onion and place the Onion over the Potatoes in the saucepan.
4. Pour Water and Tomato Sauce over Potatoes and Onions and mix together.
5. Drop Meatballs on top of Potato Mixture and bring mixture to a boil and simmer on medium low heat covered for 20 minutes.
6. When you stir mixture make sure you do not break up the Meatballs.
7. After 20 minutes, take lid off pan and let Meatballs and Potatoes simmer uncovered for 20 minutes to thicken up the sauce.

Meat Loaf

Momma always served Meat Loaf with Pinto Beans and Hominy. I never did understand how Momma could make such simple food and use only salt and pepper for seasoning. I have my own herb garden and dry my herbs but nothing I make can compare to her simple recipes.

1 pound Ground Chuck
1 small Onion chopped fine
½ Green Bell Pepper chopped fine
1 Egg
1 teaspoon Salt
1/2 teaspoon Pepper
Ketchup (enough to cover top of meatloaf)

1. Preheat oven to 350 degrees.
2. Spray a Baking Dish with Cooking Spray.
3. In a bowl mix Ground Chuck, Onion, Bell Pepper, Egg, Salt and Pepper.
4. Put in loaf pan or Pyrex dish and top with ketchup. Bake 350 until done (usually 30 to 45 minutes).

Spicy Meat Loaf

This is my version of Momma's Meat Loaf. I am no meat eater so I tend to really spice up the meat that I prepare for my husband, he loves this meat loaf.

1 pound Ground Chuck
1/2 pound Italian Pork Sausage
1 small Onion chopped fine
½ small Bell Pepper chopped fine
1/4 cup Oatmeal
2 Eggs
1/4 cup Ketchup
1 teaspoon Lawry's Season Salt
1 teaspoon McCormick Grill Mates Montreal Steak Seasoning
1/2 teaspoon Pepper
Ketchup (enough to cover top of meatloaf)

1. Preheat oven to 350 degrees.
2. Spray a Baking Dish with cooking spray.
3. In a large bowl mix Ground Chuck, Sausage, Onion, Bell Pepper and Oatmeal.
4. In a bowl beat Eggs and add Ketchup, Season Salt, Steak Seasoning, and Pepper. Add to meat mixture and mix until combined.
5. Put in Baking Dish and pour Ketchup over top.
6. Bake 45 minutes to 1 hour. Let sit about 15 minutes before eating.

*This is good using Ground Turkey and Turkey Sausage.

Fried Oysters

If the month had an 'R' in it, Momma and Daddy had Fried Oysters and Oyster Stew every Saturday night.

8 ounce container Fresh Oysters
1/2 teaspoon Salt
1/2 teaspoon Pepper
1/3 cup Corn Meal
1/4 cup Vegetable Oil

1. Heat Vegetable Oil in a Skillet over medium heat.
2. Drain water from Oysters, make sure there are no shells and place on a plate.
3. Sprinkle Salt and Pepper over Oysters.
4. Dredge Oysters in Corn Meal.
5. When Oil is hot, place Oysters in the pan and cook about 5 to 6 minutes each side until brown and cooked through.

Oyster Stew

8 ounce container Fresh Oysters
2 tablespoons Butter
12 ounce can Evaporated Milk
½ cup Water
1/8 teaspoon Salt
1/4 teaspoon Pepper

1. Heat Butter in a saucepan on medium heat.
2. Drain Oysters and take out any shells you find.
3. Place Oysters in pan with Butter and cook on medium low 4 to 5 minutes.
4. Pour Evaporated Milk and Water into pan with Oysters and season with Salt and Pepper.
5. Cook gently on medium low heat until mixture is hot. Do not let mixture come to a boil.
6. Makes 2 servings.

*You don't want to overcook your Oysters or they will become tough.

Pork Chops and Rice

6 Pork Chops
Vegetable Oil
1 can Cream of Chicken Soup
1 cup Rice
2 1/2 cups Water
1 medium Onion chopped
2 Apples, sliced

1. Brown Pork Chops in a skillet with a lid with enough Oil to just cover bottom of the pan.
2. Remove Pork Chops from skillet.
3. To skillet add Soup, Rice and Water.
4. Place Pork Chops on top then add Onions over Pork Chops.
5. Cover and cook 1 hour on low heat.
6. Add sliced Apples and cook until Apples are tender.

Pork Roast with Sweet Potatoes

2 to 2 1/2 pound Boston Butt Pork Roast
1 1/2 teaspoons Salt
1 teaspoon Pepper

3 to 4 Sweet Potatoes peeled and cut in quarters
1/2 teaspoon Salt
1/2 teaspoon Pepper

1. Preheat oven to 350 degrees.
2. Place Pork Roast in a large covered oven proof pan or place heavy duty aluminum foil in a pan (enough to cover Roast completely).
3. Sprinkle 1 1/2 teaspoons Salt and 1 teaspoon Pepper over top and bottom of Roast.
4. Cover Pork Roast and cook 1 1/2 hours.
5. Remove Roast from oven and place Sweet Potatoes around sides and sprinkle 1/2 teaspoon Salt and 1/2 teaspoon Pepper over Potatoes.
6. Return to oven and bake 1 hour.

Stuffed Pork Chops

These are not actually stuffed but Momma called them stuffed. She put the vegetables on top of the meat and baked them.

4 Pork Chops
1 medium Onion
1 large Tomato
1/2 Green Bell Pepper
1 teaspoon Salt
1 teaspoon Pepper

1. Preheat oven to 350 degrees.
2. Spray cooking spray in an oven proof pan with a lid or use heavy duty aluminum foil enough to cover meat.
3. Sprinkle Salt and Pepper over both sides of the Pork Chops.
4. Place Pork Chops in a single layer in the pan.
5. Slice Onion in 4 slices and place on top of each Pork Chop.
6. Slice the Tomato into 4 slices and place on top of the Onion.
7. Cut the Bell Pepper into 8 strips and place 2 strips on top of the Tomato.
8. Bake 1 hour to 1 hour and 15 minutes until meat is done and vegetables are tender.

Fried Pork Chops

4 Pork Chops
1 teaspoon Salt
1 teaspoon Pepper
1/2 cup Self-Rising Flour
1/2 cup Vegetable Oil

1. Place Vegetable Oil in a large skillet and place over medium heat.
2. Sprinkle Salt and Pepper over both sides of the Pork Chops.
3. Dredge Pork Chops in Flour.
4. Check the oil to make sure it is hot and place Pork Chops in skillet. Do not crowd, you may have to cook in two batches.
5. Cook the Pork Chops on medium to medium high heat about 8 to 10 minutes each side. Cook until they are brown on both sides and cooked through.

Salmon Patties

14 3/4 ounce Can Double Q Salmon
3 tablespoons finely chopped Onion
1 Egg
2 tablespoons All Purpose Flour
3 tablespoons Vegetable Oil

1. Drain Salmon, remove bones and skin, break up into pieces and place in a bowl.
2. Stir Onion and Egg into Salmon.
3. Add Flour to Salmon mixture and mix well.
4. Heat Vegetable Oil in a non-stick skillet.
5. Form Salmon into 3 inch patties and place in skillet.
6. Pan fry on medium heat until brown on both sides. About 10 minutes.
7. Makes 6 - 3 inch patties.

Swiss Steak

Momma made this recipe a lot, she served it with rice.

1 ½ pounds Round Steak or Cube Steak
2 tablespoons Vegetable Oil
1 can Campbell's Golden Mushroom Soup
½ cup chopped Canned Tomatoes
1/4 cup chopped Onion
1/4 cup Water

1. Pound Steak and cut into serving size pieces. I remember Momma doing this but now days it is easier to buy cube steak.
2. In a skillet brown steak in oil. Remove meat from skillet and pour off oil.
3. Put Steak back in skillet and add Mushroom Soup, Canned Tomatoes, Chopped Onion, and Water.
4. Simmer 1 ½ hours or until done. Stir often. Makes 4-6 servings.

Vegetables, Salads and Casseroles

Baked Beans

Momma always served Baked Beans with Fried or Barbeque Chicken and Mashed Potatoes.

15 ounce can Pork and Beans
3 tablespoons Ketchup
1 tablespoon Yellow Mustard
1/4 cup finely chopped Onion
1/4 cup finely chopped Bell Pepper
3 tablespoons Brown Sugar
1 teaspoon Worcestershire Sauce

1. Preheat oven to 350 degrees.
2. Spray a small Pyrex dish with cooking spray. I used a 6 1/2 inch square pan.
3. In a separate bowl mix Beans, Ketchup, Mustard, Onion, Bell Pepper, Brown Sugar and Worcestershire Sauce.
4. Pour into Pyrex dish.
5. Bake 35-40 minutes.

Broccoli Casserole

2 small or 1 large package of Frozen Chopped Broccoli
3 Eggs beaten
1 can Cream of Mushroom Soup
1 cup Grated Sharp Cheddar Cheese
1 cup Mayonnaise
1 medium Onion chopped
1/2 cup (1 stick) Butter or Margarine cut in small pieces
2/3 stick of Ritz crackers crushed

1. Preheat oven to 325.
2. Spray a 2 quart baking dish with cooking spray.
3. Cook Broccoli according to package directions. Drain and let cool a few minutes while you are preparing other ingredients.
4. In a medium size bowl, combine Eggs, Soup, Cheese, Mayonnaise and Onion.
5. Add cut up Butter or Margarine.
6. Stir in drained Broccoli and pour into prepared pan.
7. Top with crushed Ritz crackers.
8. Bake for 45 minutes.

Cabbage

Momma always fried up some streak o lean to serve with the cabbage.

4 cups Cabbage cut up
2 cups of Vegetable or Chicken Broth
1/2 teaspoon Salt

1. Cut Cabbage in 1 inch pieces.
2. Place Cabbage, Broth and Salt in saucepan.
3. Cook about 30 minutes until Cabbage is tender.

*I love cooked cabbage and I always use Vegetable Broth, you can use smoked salt to give the cabbage the smoky taste that meat does.

Collards or Turnip Greens

True Southern Greens are cooked with Ham, Bacon or Pork. I have included a recipe on the next page for Vegan Greens which are just as delicious.

6 cups Collards or Turnip Greens washed and torn or cut up
6 cups Water
1/2 pound Ham Hocks, Pork or Turkey Wings
2 teaspoons Salt (if your meat is very salty, reduce salt)
2 teaspoons Agave Nectar or Sugar

1. Wash Collards or Turnip Greens in a clean sink.
2. Remove tough stems and break Greens in pieces or chop on cutting board with sharp knife.
3. Place Greens in a large pan with lid and add 6 cups Water.
4. Add Meat of choice, Agave Nectar or Sugar and Salt.
5. Cook 1 to 2 hours depending on your Greens. Turnip Greens will cook faster than Collards.

Pam's Vegan Collards or Turnip Greens

6 cups Collards or Turnip Greens washed and torn or cut up
4 cups Vegetable Broth
2 cups Water
3 tablespoons Olive Oil
2 teaspoons Salt
1 small Whole Onion Peeled
2 teaspoons Agave Nectar or Sugar
1/8 teaspoon Red Pepper Flakes

1. Wash Collards or Turnip Greens in a clean sink.
2. Remove tough stems and break Greens in pieces or chop on cutting board with sharp knife.
3. Place Greens in a large pan with lid and add Vegetable Broth and Water.
4. Add Olive Oil, Salt, Onion, Agave Nectar or Sugar and Red Pepper Flakes.
5. Cook 1 to 2 hours depending on your Greens. Turnip Greens will cook faster than Collards.

*Use smoked salt instead of regular to get a smoky flavor since these are cooked with no meat.

Cheese and Macaroni

Momma always called it Cheese and Macaroni not Macaroni and Cheese! Momma's Cheese and Macaroni was not creamy. She didn't use flour, heavy cream or thickeners. Her Cheese and Macaroni was chunky pieces of cheese and macaroni, just delicious. I've never seen anyone else make it like this. Billy's daddy made Macaroni and Cheese in a similar way but he added an egg to make his stick together. I've included his recipe on the next page.

8 ounce box Macaroni cooked in salted water until al dente
2 cups Sharp Cheddar Cheese
2 cups Milk
2 tablespoons Butter or Margarine
1/4 teaspoon Salt
1/4 teaspoon Pepper

1. Preheat Oven to 350 degrees and spray a 2 quart oven proof dish with cooking spray.
2. Drain cooked Macaroni and put half of it in a 2 quart oven proof dish.
3. Slice Cheese into 1/4 inch pieces about 2 inches long and place Cheese over Macaroni.
4. Place the other half of the Macaroni over the Cheese.
5. Dot with pieces of Butter or Margarine.
6. Measure Milk into a 2 cup measure and stir in Salt and Pepper.
7. Pour Milk mixture over Cheese and Macaroni.
8. Bake at 350 until bubbly about 30-35 minutes.
9. Let sit about 5 minutes before serving.

Mr. Hudson's Macaroni and Cheese

8 ounce box Macaroni cooked in salted water until al dente
1 pound of Medium Cheddar Cheese Grated
2 cups Milk
1 Egg
2 tablespoons Butter or Margarine
1/4 teaspoon Salt
1/4 teaspoon Pepper

1. Preheat Oven to 350 degrees and spray a 2 quart oven proof dish with cooking spray.
2. Drain cooked Macaroni and put it in a 2 quart oven proof dish.
3. Stir Grated Cheese into Macaroni.
4. Dot with pieces of Butter or Margarine.
5. Measure Milk into a 2 cup measure and add Beaten Egg, Salt and Pepper.
6. Pour Milk mixture over Cheese and Macaroni and stir together.
7. Bake at 350 20-30 minutes.
8. Let sit about 5 minutes before serving.

Cole Slaw

Momma always wanted me to make the slaw because she said mine was better. I think she didn't want to grate the cabbage.

4 cups Grated Cabbage (about 1/2 of a large head of cabbage)
2 small or 1 large Carrot grated
1/4 cup Sweet Salad Cube Pickles
1/4 cup Mayonnaise
1 tablespoon Apple Cider Vinegar
1 tablespoon Dijon Mustard
1/2 teaspoon Celery Seed
1 teaspoon Sugar
1/2 teaspoon Salt
1/4 teaspoon Pepper

1. Grate Cabbage and Carrots and place in large bowl.
2. Add Sweet Pickles to Cabbage and Carrots and stir together.
3. In a small bowl, combine Mayonnaise, Vinegar, Mustard, Celery Seed, Sugar, Salt and Pepper.
4. Pour dressing over Cabbage mixture and mix until all are combined.

*To make Vegan, use Vegenaise instead of Mayonnaise.
**When Vidalia Onions are in season, I make an Onion Slaw. I use Cabbage and about 2 tablespoons grated Vidalia Onions, Mayonnaise, Salt and Pepper. Cole Slaw is so versatile, you can use dill pickles instead of sweet and leave out the Mustard and Vinegar altogether.

Corn Casserole

2 - 14 1/2 ounce cans Whole Kernel Corn drained
1/4 cup Sugar
1 1/2 tablespoons All Purpose Flour
1/2 teaspoon Salt
1/2 teaspoon Pepper
1/2 pint Heavy Cream
1/4 cup Butter or Margarine

1. Preheat oven to 350 degrees.
2. Spray a 1 1/2 to 2 quart baking dish with cooking spray.
3. Place Corn in baking dish.
4. Mix together Sugar, Flour, Salt and Pepper and mix into Corn.
5. Pour Heavy Cream over Corn mixture.
6. Cut Butter or Margarine into chunks and place on top.
7. Bake 35 minutes and stir twice while baking.

*You can use 2 pints of fresh corn instead of canned corn.

Cream Corn

In the South, we always look forward to the Silver Queen Corn that is available in July. My favorite summer treat is a Vine Ripe Tomato sliced, cut up and seasoned with Salt and Pepper and covered in Cream Corn.

6 ears of Fresh Corn
1/4 cup Butter or Margarine (1/2 stick)
1/2 teaspoon Salt
1/2 teaspoon Pepper
3/4 to 1 cup Water

1. Shuck Corn and wash ears of corn to get all the silks off.
2. Cut off kernels about half way and then scrape the ears of Corn into a bowl. You will have the corn kernels and the creamy milk from the corn.
3. Transfer Corn to a non-stick skillet.
4. Add Butter or Margarine, Salt, Pepper and Water.
5. Cook on low heat for about 30 minutes, stirring occasionally. Make sure corn doesn't stick to pan. If you need more water add a little at a time.

*You could reduce the water to 1/2 cup to make a creamier corn. Just be sure to stir and reduce cooking time to 15 minutes.

Creamed Potatoes

Some people say Mashed Potatoes, Momma called them Creamed Potatoes and they were a staple at our house.

4 cups Irish Potatoes peeled and cut up in slices or cubes
5 cups Cold Water (enough to cover Potatoes in saucepan)
2 tablespoons Butter or Margarine
1/2 cup Milk
1 teaspoon Salt
1/2 teaspoon Pepper

1. Place Potatoes and Water in a saucepan. Bring water to boil and cook 10-15 minutes until Potatoes are fork tender.
2. Drain water from Potatoes.
3. Using a hand held electric mixer, combine Potatoes, Butter or Margarine, Milk, Salt and Pepper and beat until everything is combined and Potatoes are smooth.

*To make Vegan, use Non-Dairy Milk and Margarine.

Deviled Eggs

We always had Potato Salad with the Deviled Eggs. I Remember Momma using her Potato Salad Deviled Egg Bowl. It was so pretty.

6 Boiled Eggs
2 tablespoons Mayonnaise
2 teaspoons Yellow Mustard
2 tablespoons Sweet Pickles diced or Sweet Salad Cubes
1/4 teaspoon Salt
1/4 teaspoon Pepper
Paprika

1. Place Eggs in a small pan with enough cold water to cover and 1 tablespoon Salt.
2. Place pan with Eggs on stove to cook. When the water starts boiling, cover and remove from heat.
3. Let pan of Eggs sit 15 minutes and do not open lid. After 15 minutes remove Eggs from the pan and set aside to cool. Carefully remove shells from eggs.
4. Cut Eggs in half and take out yellow of egg and place in a bowl. Put Egg Whites on the dish you plan to serve in.
5. Mash yellow of Egg and add Mayonnaise, Mustard, Sweet Pickles, Salt and Pepper and mix together.
6. Spoon Mixture into each Egg White, sprinkle with Paprika and Serve.

*Momma liked to use the sandwich spread that contained pickles instead of Mayonnaise, Mustard and Pickles.

Dried Beans

To say dried beans were a staple in our house is an understatement. To this day, I love any kind of dried bean. We ate them because they were economical and easy to prepare. I found heirloom dried beans which are quite expensive and Momma would be shocked to know how much I paid for them. Momma made a different dried bean every day and had her menu to go with each bean. If you saw Pinto Beans soaking, you knew you would have Meat Loaf for supper.

Dried Beans are easy so don't be intimidated with the soaking and long cook times. You can put them on and let them cook stirring occasionally and adding more water if needed or cook them in a pressure cooker.

1. Beans usually double in volume but some triple. So usually 1 cup dried beans equals 2 cups cooked.
2. For an overnight soak, wash and sort beans, place in a large bowl with 6 cups of water per pound of beans. Let stand overnight.
3. For a quick soak, wash and sort beans. Put beans and water in a large saucepan and bring water to boil and cook 2 minutes. Remove from heat, cover and let stand 1 hour.
4. Drain Beans and add fresh water for cooking.
5. Beans usually take 1 to 1 1/2 hours to cook, less time using a pressure cooker.

Cooking Dried Beans

Momma Buttram's favorite dried beans were Large Lima Beans, Baby Lima Beans, Pinto Beans, Black Eyed Peas and Great Northern Beans.

1. Wash, sort and soak 1 cup of dried beans overnight. I place a pinch of baking soda in the soaking water to help take some of the gas out of the beans.
2. Drain and rinse beans and place in a saucepan with enough fresh water to cover the beans.
3. Bring the beans and water to a boil. Skim off the foam that covers the top of the water. Add a pinch of baking soda which will cause more foam and skim that off. This helps to take out the gas from the beans.
4. To the beans and water, add 1 teaspoon Salt, 1 tablespoon Olive Oil (Olive Oil is optional) and a Bouillon Cube of your choice and a whole peeled Onion. I use a Vegetable Bouillon Cube but you can use Chicken or Beef. Momma seasoned her beans with pork fat back. If you use fat back be sure to rinse off the salt. You can also use bacon or ham. If using meat, you do not need to add the olive oil.
5. Cook the beans on low in a covered pan at a slow boil. Stir occasionally and add more water as needed.

Pam's Black Beans

This is the recipe I use for all of my dried beans except for the Cilantro. I like the taste of the Cilantro with the Black Beans served with Brown Rice of course.

1 cup dried Black Beans
6 cups Water
1/4 teaspoon Baking Soda Divided (1/8 for soaking and 1/8 for cooking)
1 Vegetable Bouillon Cube
1/2 cup fresh chopped Cilantro
1 tablespoon Olive Oil (optional)
1 small whole Onion peeled
1 teaspoon Salt

1. The night before you cook the beans, wash and soak beans in water with 1/8 teaspoon Baking Soda.
2. The next day, drain the soaking water and discard.
3. Put Black Beans in a saucepan and add 6 cups of water.
4. Let Beans come to a boil and skim off the foam that forms on top.
5. Add 1/8 teaspoon Baking Soda and skim off the foam that forms from adding the Baking Soda.
6. Add the Bouillon Cube, Cilantro, Olive Oil, Onion and Salt.
7. Place lid on pan and let Beans simmer on medium low heat for 1 1/2 to 2 hours until beans are tender. Add more water if needed.

*You could use 4 cups of Vegetable Broth and 2 cups of Water instead of the 6 cups of Water and Bouillon Cube if desired.

English Peas

We never had Creamed Potatoes without English Peas. I always put the Creamed Potatoes on my plate and made a well for the English Peas to go on top. Daddy grew fresh peas in the spring, they were so delicious. If you are lucky enough to find fresh peas, cook them the same way with a little water until tender.

1 can English Peas
1/4 cup Butter or Margarine

1. Place English Peas in saucepan and add Butter or Margarine.
2. Heat and serve.

Green Beans

The trick to true southern green beans is to cook them. Southerners do not eat crunchy green beans. Sorry, I know about the vitamins that are lost but these are sooooo good.

4 cups Fresh Green Beans
2 tablespoons Bacon Grease or small slice of Fatback
Enough water to top of beans but do not cover beans
1 teaspoon Salt
1/2 teaspoon Pepper

1. Wash Green Beans, take strings off and snap into 1 inch pieces.
2. Put Green Beans in a 2 quart saucepan and add water but do not cover Beans in water.
3. Add Bacon Grease or Fatback Meat, Salt and Pepper.
4. Cook 1 hour stirring occasionally. Watch water and add if needed. You probably won't need to. Adjust Salt and Pepper if needed.

Pam's Green Beans

This is my vegan version of Momma's Green Beans.

4 cups Fresh Green Beans
1 tablespoon Olive Oil
1 Vegetable Bouillon Cube
1 small whole Onion peeled
1 teaspoon Salt
1/2 teaspoon Pepper
Enough water to top of beans but do not cover beans

1. Wash Green Beans and take all strings off the Beans and snap into 1 inch pieces.
2. Put Green Beans in a 2 quart saucepan and add water but do not cover Beans in water.
3. Add Olive Oil, Bouillon Cube, Onion, Salt and Pepper.
4. Cook 1 hour stirring occasionally. Watch water and add if needed. You probably won't need to. Adjust Salt and Pepper if needed.

Fried Okra

Momma had a friend who lived in Anniston, AL. We visited her one summer and for lunch she went out to her backyard and picked some okra, went in the kitchen and fried them up. Best okra I ever ate.

2 cups Fresh Okra cut up
2 tablespoons Corn Meal
1/2 teaspoon Salt
6 tablespoons Vegetable Oil or enough to cover bottom of skillet

1. Cut stems off of Okra and cut in 1/2 to 3/4 inch rounds.
2. Put Okra in a bowl and add Corn Meal and Salt, stirring to coat Okra in Meal.
3. Heat Oil in a skillet.
4. When Oil is hot, add Okra. Put enough Okra in pan to cover bottom of pan. Don't crowd the pan, you may have to fry in two batches.
5. Pan fry Okra on medium high heat for about 15 minutes or until brown on both sides.
6. Place on a plate lined with paper towels to absorb the oil.

*If you have a Green Tomato, dice it up and fry with the Okra, you will need to add another tablespoon of Corn Meal.

Okra and Tomatoes

2 tablespoons Vegetable Oil
1/2 cup chopped Onion
1 cup sliced Okra cut in 1/2 to 3/4 inch pieces
1 cup Tomato diced (about 1 large tomato)
1/2 teaspoon Salt
1/2 teaspoon Pepper

1. Heat Vegetable Oil in small saucepan.
2. Add Onion to Oil and cook 5 minutes.
3. Add Okra, Tomato, Salt and Pepper to Onion in pan.
4. Cook 30 minutes until everything is stewed together.
5. You will not need to add water because the water in the tomato should be enough liquid.

Pear Salad

What can I say about Pear Salad except if you have never had it you are missing out on a delicious Southern treat! It is so cool and refreshing in the summer for a light lunch. Momma made Pear Salad very often. My Aunt Mildred always made a large plate of it for our Jordan Family Reunions and served the Pear Salad with Ritz Crackers. The family reunions were held at Uncle Ralph and Aunt Mildred's house in the country where there was enough food for an army, horseback riding and ice cold water from the spring with a view of the mountains and countryside that is forever lost to time.

15 ounce can Pear Halves in Heavy Syrup
Mayonnaise
1 cup grated Cheese
Iceberg or Green Leaf Lettuce
Maraschino Cherries

1. Drain Pear halves and set aside.
2. Place Lettuce leaves on a large plate.
3. Place a Pear half in the center of Lettuce leaves.
4. Place about 1 teaspoon Mayonnaise in the center of each Pear half.
5. Sprinkle grated Cheese over each Pear half.
6. Top each Pear half with a Maraschino Cherry.

*There are usually 6 Pear halves in each 15 ounce can. You can add more Mayonnaise or Cheese as desired.

Hot Pepper Sauce

This is a very Hot Pepper Sauce so if you don't like it hot, make the Pepper Sauce recipe.

3 cups Jalapeno Peppers sliced
2 cups Vinegar
1 cup Sugar
1 teaspoon Salt

1. Wearing plastic gloves, cut Jalapeno Peppers in half and remove seeds and membrane.
2. Cut halved Jalapeno Peppers into slices.
3. Heat Vinegar, Sugar and Salt in a saucepan and bring to a boil.
4. Add sliced Jalapeno Peppers and cook 3 to 4 minutes longer.
5. Pour into jars. Makes about 4 cups of Pepper Sauce.

Pepper Sauce

This is the easiest and best Pepper Sauce, it isn't too hot and really compliments greens. It's hard to formulate a recipe for this so I've just advised what to do.

**Hot peppers such as Jalapeno, Cayenne, Chili Peppers or
    Cow Horns to fill a quart jar
4 cups White Vinegar**

1. Wash and dry peppers and place in a quart jar with tight fitting lid.
2. Heat White Vinegar to almost boiling.
3. Pour Vinegar over Peppers in the jar and seal.

*We never have Turnip or Collard Greens without Pepper Sauce.

Fried Irish Potatoes

A Momma Buttram Biscuit filled with Fried Irish Potatoes is so delicious! We were dog sitting a friend's large Labrador. Momma, Daddy and I were sitting around the supper table enjoying another one of Momma's delicious meals. Daddy looked around and saw the dog eating a biscuit. He said, "Evelyn, did you give that dog a biscuit"? She looked around and saw him eating it and said, "No, I didn't give it to him". The biscuits always sat on the corner of the table between Momma and Daddy, the dog just made himself at home and took a biscuit.

4 Irish Potatoes Peeled and Sliced
Canola Oil, enough to cover bottom of non-stick skillet

1. Heat Oil in skillet.
2. Add Potatoes and cook on medium heat, until tender and brown on both sides. Don't crowd the pan.
3. Drain on a paper towel and season with Salt .

Potatoes in White Sauce

This was one of Momma's specialties, everyone loved them especially my best friend Cindy. I had not made these in years so I formulated the recipe for a Sunday Dinner for me and my husband. I decided that the first bite from my plate would be the Potatoes in White Sauce. When the potatoes hit my tongue, a feeling came over me and I was taken back to Momma's table. They tasted just like hers and I took a deep breath and fought back the tears. That is what food does for us, it immediately takes you back to a time, place and people that you love.

Potatoes
4 to 5 cups Potatoes peeled and cubed
Water to cover Potatoes in saucepan
1/2 teaspoon Salt

White Sauce
1/2 cup Potato Water
2 tablespoons Self-Rising Flour
1/2 cup Milk
1 tablespoon Butter or Margarine
1/2 teaspoon Salt
1/4 teaspoon Pepper

1. Peel and cube Potatoes and place in a large saucepan with enough cold water to cover the Potatoes. Add 1/2 teaspoon Salt.
2. Let Potatoes come to a boil, reduce heat and cook about 10 minutes until Potatoes are tender.
3. Using a slotted spoon, place the Potatoes in a large bowl.
4. Reserve 1/2 cup of the Potato Water and put it in the saucepan and discard the remainder of the Potato Water.
5. Place Flour and Milk in a jar with a tight fitting lid and shake until no lumps are seen.
6. Pour Flour and Milk mixture into the Potato Water and place on medium heat and stir to combine.
7. Add Potatoes, Butter or Margarine, Salt and Pepper to mixture and cook on low to medium heat stirring constantly until thick.
8. You can add more milk if you need more liquid but the mixture should be very thick.

Warm Potato Salad

This is the only Potato Salad Recipe I have ever seen that called for apples. It is delicious served warm. This was the only Potato Salad that Momma made.

5 cups Diced Potatoes - about 5 medium
2 Eggs Hard Boiled chopped
1 small Apple cut up into pieces about the size of the potatoes
1/4 cup Sweet Pickle cut up or Sweet Salad Cubes
1/4 cup Mayonnaise
1/2 to 1 teaspoon Salt to taste

1. Place Eggs in a small pan with enough cold water to cover and 1 tablespoon Salt.
2. Place pan with Eggs on stove to cook. When the water starts boiling, cover and remove from heat.
3. Let pan of Eggs sit 15 minutes and do not open lid. After 15 minutes remove Eggs from the pan and set aside to cool.
4. Peel and dice Potatoes. Place Potatoes in a pan and cover with cold water and 1 teaspoon Salt.
5. Let water come to a boil and turn down just until it is at a low boil and cook about 10 minutes until potatoes are tender but not mushy.
6. Drain Potatoes in a colander and let cool slightly.
7. Add Eggs, Sweet Pickles, Apple, Salt and Mayonnaise.
8. Serve WARM

*If you don't like apples in your Potato Salad, leave them out.

Pam's Potato Salad

This Potato Salad is better served cold and is really delicious the next day.

5 cups Diced Potatoes around 5 medium
3 Hard Boiled Eggs
2 teaspoons Grated Onion
1/4 cup Dill Pickle chopped or Dill Salad Cubes
3 tablespoons or 12 Pimento Stuffed Green Olives chopped
1/2 to 1 teaspoon Celery Seed
1 teaspoon Lawry's Season Salt
2 ounce Jar of Diced Pimentos
1/4 cup Mayonnaise
2 tablespoons Yellow Mustard
1/4 teaspoon Pepper
Paprika

1. Place Eggs in a small pan with enough cold water to cover and 1 tablespoon Salt.
2. Place pan with Eggs on stove to cook. When the water starts boiling, cover and remove from heat.
3. Let pan of Eggs sit 15 minutes and do not open lid. After 15 minutes remove Eggs from the pan and set aside to cool.
4. Peel and dice Potatoes. Place Potatoes in a pan and cover with cold water and 1 teaspoon Salt.
5. Let water come to a boil and turn down just until it is at a low boil and cook about 10 minutes until Potatoes are tender but not mushy.
6. Drain Potatoes in a colander and let cool completely.
7. Using a box grater slice Eggs on slicer side and grate Onion on grater side. Add to Potatoes.
8. To Potato mixture, add Pickles, Olives, Celery Seed, Lawry's Season Salt, Pimentos, Mayonnaise, Mustard and Pepper. Stir to combine.
9. Place in bowl and sprinkle Paprika on top.
10. This potato salad is better made the day before and served cold.

*You can wash the potatoes, leave them whole and the skin on them and cook in water until they are tender. Let Potatoes cool to the touch, peel and cut in cubes.

Rutabaga

A definite staple in the South, Rutabaga Turnips are so delicious especially with Corn Bread.

1 medium Rutabaga (about 6 to 7 cups) peeled, sliced and cut in small pieces
4 cups Vegetable Broth
1 teaspoon Salt
1/2 teaspoon Pepper
1 tablespoon Olive Oil
2 tablespoons Agave Nectar or Sugar
2 tablespoons Apple Cider Vinegar

1. Place Rutabaga in a heavy pan with lid. I use a cast iron Brazier Pot which works perfectly.
2. To the pot, add Broth, Salt, Pepper, Olive Oil, Agave Nectar or Sugar and Vinegar.
3. Bring to a boil and reduce heat and cover and cook 1 1/2 hours or until fork tender. Add water if needed but you want most of the liquid to cook out.
4. When done, mash with a potato masher.

Squash Casserole

Even the best cooks make mistakes. Momma had cooked a meal for us and I invited a boyfriend to dinner. She made delicious sweet tea but that night she set the glasses on the table and said, "I don't know what is wrong with the tea, it looks there are grounds in it". My boyfriend said, "I think I'll have water". Momma had used coffee instead of her usual loose tea leaves.

2 to 2 1/2 pounds Yellow Squash cut in 2 inch pieces
1/2 cup Sour Cream
1/4 cup Butter or Margarine, melted
1/4 cup Onion chopped
1/2 teaspoon Salt
1/4 teaspoon Pepper
1/2 cup Bread or Cracker Crumbs

1. Preheat oven to 350 degrees.
2. Cook Yellow Squash in a little water until tender.
3. Drain Squash and place in a medium size bowl.
4. Add Sour Cream, Melted Butter or Margarine, Onion, Salt and Pepper and mix well.
5. Lightly grease a 1 quart baking dish. Pour Squash mixture into baking dish.
6. Sprinkle Bread or Cracker Crumbs over top and bake 25 minutes until bubbly.

Fried Squash

4 cups of Yellow Squash Sliced
2 to 3 tablespoons Corn Meal
1 teaspoon Salt
6 tablespoons Vegetable Oil

1. Wash and slice Yellow Squash.
2. Place Squash in a bowl and add Corn Meal and Salt. Stir together until all of the Squash is coated with Corn Meal.
3. Heat Vegetable Oil in a skillet and when it is hot, add the Squash making sure that you only have one layer of squash. You will have to fry in a couple of batches.
4. Cook on medium high heat 3 to 5 minutes each side until both sides are golden brown.
5. Place on a plate lined with paper towels to absorb the oil.

Stewed Squash

2 cups Yellow Squash sliced
1/2 to 3/4 cups chopped Onion
1/2 teaspoon Salt
1/4 teaspoon Pepper
3 tablespoons Vegetable Oil or Bacon Grease
Water

1. Wash and slice Yellow Squash, set aside.
2. Chop Onion and sauté in a skillet with Vegetable Oil or Bacon Grease for about 5 minutes.
3. Place Yellow Squash in skillet with onions. Add Salt and Pepper and Stir together.
4. Add 4 tablespoons water and cook until water is absorbed and add 4 tablespoons more water. Add water 4 tablespoons at a time as needed until Squash is tender about 30 minutes.

Candied Sweet Potatoes

I've never seen anyone make Sweet Potatoes like this. The recipes I found call for the candied potatoes to be baked in the oven or made into a casserole. Momma made these in the fall when Sweet Potatoes were fresh.

4 cups Sweet Potatoes peeled and sliced (about 4 medium Sweet Potatoes)
1/4 cup Butter or Margarine (1/2 stick)
1/2 cup Sugar

1. Peel and slice Sweet Potatoes.
2. Heat Butter or Margarine in a skillet (cast iron works best).
3. Place Sweet Potatoes in melted Butter or Margarine.
4. Sprinkle Potatoes with Sugar.
5. Cook on medium to medium low heat for 30-40 minutes turning potatoes frequently. You want the potatoes to get soft and caramelized, you don't want to brown or fry the potatoes.

Marinated Vegetable Salad

17 ounce can English Peas, drained
17 ounce can White Shoe Peg Corn, drained
15 ounce can French Style Green Beans, drained
2 ounce jar diced Pimento, drained
1/2 cup diced Celery
1/2 cup chopped Green Bell Pepper
1/2 cup chopped Onion
1 cup Sugar
1 teaspoon Salt
1/2 teaspoon Pepper
1/2 cup Vegetable Oil
3/4 cup White Vinegar

1. Combine English Peas, Corn, Green Beans, Pimento, Celery, Bell Pepper, and Onion in a large bowl.
2. In a saucepan put Sugar, Salt, Pepper, Oil and Vinegar and bring to a boil over low heat.
3. Pour over Vegetables and stir gently.
4. Refrigerate for 24 hours before serving.

Zucchini Casserole

1 1/2 pounds Zucchini Squash
3 tablespoons Butter or Margarine
1/2 cup diced Green Bell Pepper
1/2 cup chopped Onion
3 large chopped Tomatoes
3 tablespoons All Purpose Flour
1 1/2 teaspoons Salt
1/2 teaspoon Pepper
1/2 cup Buttered Bread Crumbs
1/4 cup Grated Cheese
1 teaspoon Sugar

1. Preheat oven to 350 degrees.
2. Spray a 2 quart baking dish with cooking spray.
3. Wash and slice Squash and cook in a small amount of water in covered pan for 8 minutes.
4. Drain Squash and place in casserole dish.
5. Melt Butter or Margarine in a skillet and sauté Green Pepper and Onion until limp, but not brown.
6. Add Tomatoes and sprinkle with Flour and stir well. Cook 2 or 3 minutes until vegetables are tender.
7. Season with Salt, Pepper and Sugar. Spoon mixture over Squash.
8. Combine Buttered Bread Crumbs and Grated Cheese. Sprinkle over casserole.
9. Bake 30 minutes.

Breads

Momma Buttram's Biscuits

Momma made biscuits twice a day. She got up with Daddy at 5:30am and made biscuits for breakfast. She made enough biscuits so that he could take them to work. He did not like loaf bread and Momma's biscuits held together just like bread. If it was just after payday, he would take biscuits with ham or sausage. If it was close to payday, he would take biscuits with butter and jelly or cheese. She then made a fresh batch for supper. She made her biscuits with Lard until Daddy had his first heart attack and the Cardiologist made her switch to Crisco.

4 cups Self-Rising Flour
1/3 cup Crisco or Lard if you are brave
3/4 cup Milk or Dry Milk Powder mixed with water (Made-up milk)

I can tell you how she made them. I promise if you try this and practice you can do it. It's not rocket science, it's biscuits. Oh and let them feel the love, they know if you are scared!

1. Preheat Oven to 475 degrees.
2. Sift Self-Rising Flour in a large bowl and make a well in the center. You will not use all the flour.
3. Put 1/3 cup Crisco in the well.
4. Work the Crisco together with a little Flour but keep it in the well. You are basically just cutting a little Flour and Crisco together.
5. Add "made-up milk", a little at a time to form a sticky dough and again keep it in the well. Using your hand as a claw, mix the Crisco, Flour and Milk adding a little bit of flour at a time.
6. Knead the dough (still in the well) incorporating flour so it would not be sticky but will take on a very smooth consistency.
7. Wash your hands and then with a little flour on your hands, break off a small amount of dough and roll it into a ball. Place the ball on a greased cookie sheet and press it down with the back of your fingers. Makes about 8 biscuits. Save Flour that is left in bowl to use for next batch.
8. Bake 10-12 minutes or until brown.

I hear people on cooking shows say "Don't work the dough too much so it will be flakey". Well, Momma's biscuits were not flakey, they were more the consistency of bread. They would hold up to anything and they were wonderful!

She used her biscuit dough to make cobblers and chicken or pork with dumplings.

Biscuits for 'Scardy Cats'

2 cups sifted Self-Rising Flour
1/4 cup Shortening
about 3/4 cup milk

1. Preheat oven to 425 degrees.
2. Sift Flour into a large bowl.
3. Cut in Shortening.
4. Add Milk gradually, stirring until soft dough is formed.
5. Turn out on slightly floured board and lightly "knead" for 30 seconds, enough to shape.
6. Roll dough 1/2 to 3/4 inch thick and cut with 2 inch floured biscuit cutter.
7. Bake on ungreased baking sheet for 10-12 minutes or until brown.
8. Makes 10-12 biscuits.

*For flakier biscuits, use Butter Milk.

Corn Bread

Momma used Perkerson's Corn Meal which was coarse and made a substantial corn bread. We never used a recipe. We heated the iron skillet with some oil, poured corn meal into a bowl and added 1 egg and milk (buttermilk or plain) and after combining we added the hot oil.

2 cups Corn Meal mix
1 ¼ to 1 ½ cups Buttermilk
¼ cup Vegetable Oil
1 Egg

1. Preheat Oven to 425 degrees.
2. Put Oil in a 10 inch Iron Skillet and heat while you are mixing up corn bread mixture.
3. Mix Corn Meal mix, Buttermilk and Egg together.
4. Add hot Oil to mixture leaving a small amount in skillet.
5. Pour Corn Bread mixture into hot skillet and bake 20-25 minutes until golden brown.

*If you make Corn Bread, you have to use an Iron Skillet. They are not expensive and you can find them at most hardware stores.
**When you use a Corn Meal mix, you don't need to add Salt and Baking Soda.

Mexican Cornbread

1 cup Yellow Corn Meal
1/2 teaspoon Salt
1/2 teaspoon Baking Soda
1/3 cup Vegetable Oil
2 Eggs beaten
1 cup Cream Style Corn
2/3 cup Buttermilk
1 cup grated Cheddar Cheese
1 small can chopped Green Chili Peppers

1. Preheat oven to 300 degrees.
2. Heat oil in a 10-12 inch cast iron skillet.
3. In a bowl mix Corn Meal, Salt and Soda.
4. Stir in Eggs, Corn, and Buttermilk and mix well.
5. Add hot Oil leaving about a tablespoon in skillet and stir until combined.
6. Pour one half of the mixture into the hot skillet and sprinkle cheese and peppers over the mixture and cover with other half of the Corn meal mixture.
7. Bake 30 to 40 minutes.

*If you use a Corn Meal Mix, omit the Salt and Baking Soda.

Desserts

Cake Pan Preparation

This is a tip I got from my friend Sharon. I keep this in a jar in my refrigerator at all times so it is ready when I decide to make a cake.

1/2 cup Crisco
1/2 cup Vegetable Oil
1/2 cup All Purpose Flour

1. Cream Crisco and Vegetable Oil together.
2. Add Flour and beat until no lumps are seen.
3. Pour into a jar and use when recipe calls for you to grease and flour cake pans.

*I love this because I used to get flour all over my kitchen when I greased and floured the cake pans.

Momma Buttram's Ambrosia

We ALWAYS had Ambrosia at Christmas with Momma's delicious cakes.

6 Oranges peeled and sectioned
Juice from the 6 Oranges
15 ounce can crushed Pineapple
10 ounce jar Maraschino Cherries
3 Apples peeled and diced
3 Bananas cut in small pieces
2 tablespoons Sugar to taste

1. Peel, section and squeeze juice from Oranges into a large bowl.
2. Add Pineapple, Cherries, Apples, Bananas and Sugar.
3. Stir and taste, add more sugar if needed depending on sweetness of fruit.

*You may need more oranges depending on how big the oranges are. This is a recipe that you can add other kinds of fruit or leave out anything you don't like.

Apple Pie

Think Apple Pecan Pie, this pie is so delicious and with the cloves it reminds me of Thanksgiving and Christmas. This pie will freeze well so you can make it ahead, just let it thaw and heat in the oven just before serving.

2 cups Grated Apples
1 ½ cups Sugar
1 stick Butter or Margarine melted
3 Eggs beaten
1/4 teaspoon Cinnamon
1/8 teaspoon Nutmeg
1/2 teaspoon Cloves
1 cup chopped Pecans or Walnuts
1 Unbaked Pie Shell

1. Preheat oven to 350 degrees.
2. In a large bowl combine grated Apples, Sugar, melted Butter or Margarine, beaten Eggs, Cinnamon, Nutmeg, Cloves and Nuts.
3. Pour into the Unbaked Pie Shell.
4. Cook 60-65 minutes until pie is set and golden brown on top.
5. Serve warm with Vanilla Ice Cream.

Apple Pies

Momma made these at least once a month, she always had dried apples in the cabinet.

8 ounces Dried Apples
3 cups Water
1/2 cup Sugar
1 teaspoon Cinnamon
1 recipe Momma Buttram's Biscuits (Pages 71, 72)
1/4 cup Margarine or Butter melted

1. Cook Apples, Water, Sugar and Cinnamon for 30 minutes until apples are tender. The mixture should be very thick with no liquid left in the pan.
2. Set Apple mixture aside and let cool completely.
3. Preheat oven to 375 degrees and spray a baking sheet with cooking spray.
4. Prepare Biscuit Recipe.
5. Make 8 equal balls with Biscuit dough.
6. On a floured surface, roll each ball into a 5 inch round.
7. Place 2 tablespoons of the Apple mixture on one side of the dough and fold remaining dough over, it will look like a half moon.
8. Crimp edges of dough with a fork to keep pie closed.
9. Place on baking sheet and continue making pies.
10. Using a fork punch tops of pies three times to vent.
11. Spoon melted Butter or Margarine over each pie.
12. Bake 20-25 minutes until golden brown.

*Any leftover apples are good by themselves or on top of oatmeal for breakfast.

Old Fashioned Baked Apples

I remember Momma's Baked Apples. This was an easy dessert and when apples were in season we had them often. The first recipe is how Momma usually made them, plain and old fashioned with sugar crystals on top. The next recipe is one Momma found and started making a little fancier.

6 large Apples
1/2 cup Sugar
6 tablespoons Butter
Cinnamon to sprinkle over apples, as much as you like
Water

1. Preheat oven to 350 degrees. Spray a Pyrex dish large enough for apples to fit in one layer with cooking spray.
2. Cut the top and bottom from each Apple (Momma never cored her apples, you just ate around the seeds).
3. Place Apples in the Pyrex dish.
4. On top of apple put Butter or Margarine, Sugar and Cinnamon (as much as you can). Pour a little Water (about 1 cup) in dish.
5. Bake 350 degrees until Apples are tender (start checking after 30 minutes of cooking).

Honey Baked Apples

6 large apples
3 tablespoons chopped Walnuts
3 tablespoons Raisins
1 cup Water
1/3 cup Honey
1 3-inch Stick Cinnamon
1 tablespoon Lemon Juice

1. Preheat Oven to 350 degrees.
2. Core Apples and peel top third of each.
3. Place Apples in a shallow baking dish. Combine Walnuts and Raisins and stuff cavities of Apple with nut mixture.
4. Combine Water, Honey and Cinnamon Stick in a small saucepan. Bring to a boil, reduce heat then simmer 5 minutes. Remove from heat, stir in Lemon Juice. Remove Cinnamon Stick.
5. Pour liquid over Apples.
6. Cover and bake at 350 for 45 to 50 minutes or until Apples are tender basting occasionally.

Banana Pudding

Please don't use instant pudding for your Banana Pudding. It only takes a few more minutes to make real pudding. Momma sometimes made Strawberry or Pineapple pudding instead of Banana.

3/4 cups Sugar
1/3 cup All Purpose Flour or Cornstarch
Dash Salt
4 Eggs Separated
12 ounce can Evaporated Milk
3/4 cup Milk
1/2 teaspoon Vanilla
3 Sliced Bananas or 2 cups
12 ounce Box Vanilla Wafers
3 tablespoons Sugar for the Meringue

1. Preheat oven to 350 degrees.
2. In a double boiler put Sugar, Flour or Cornstarch and Salt and mix together.
3. Add the Egg Yolks and stir together.
4. Add Evaporated Milk and Milk. Cook in double boiler until it thickens.
5. Remove from heat and add Vanilla.
6. Beat Egg Whites until stiff peaks form and add 3 tablespoons Sugar.
7. Slice Bananas and layer with Vanilla Wafers in a 9X9 inch Pyrex dish.
8. Pour pudding over the top of the layered Bananas and Wafers.
9. Top with beaten Egg Whites and place in 350 degree oven for about 15 minutes or until meringue is brown.

*If you feel you need more custard, increase sugar to 1 cup and cornstarch by 1 tablespoon and add about a ½ cup more milk.

Strawberry Pudding

Use same recipe as Banana Pudding with 2 cups fresh strawberries instead of bananas.

Pineapple Pudding

Use same recipe as Banana Pudding with 2 cups canned crushed pineapple instead of bananas.

Blueberry Cobbler

Momma got this recipe from Luna Belle Buttram. Lois Jordan and Luna Belle Buttram were Daddy's sisters who lived in Cedartown, GA. They both retired from the Goodyear Mill in Cedartown and lived together as long as I knew them. They were the best cooks in the world. No matter what they put on the table, it tasted better than anything you ever had. I remember spending the night with them and for breakfast we had cereal, toast and grapefruit and that was the best breakfast I ever ate.

4 cups Blueberries
3/4 cup Sugar
3/4 cup Water
1 teaspoon Lemon Juice

Topping
1 stick Butter softened
1 ½ cups Self-Rising Flour
1 cup Sugar

1. Preheat oven to 350 degrees.
2. Grease a 10 inch pan with cooking spray.
3. Combine Blueberries, Sugar and Water in a large bowl.
4. Stir Lemon Juice into Berry mixture.
5. Place Berry mixture in baking pan.
6. To prepare topping, mix Butter, Flour and Sugar with pastry blender until it is consistency of meal.
7. Spread topping on Berries.
8. Bake for about 25 to 30 minutes.

Caramel Cake

Momma was a great detective. She only had a telephone and the newspaper and she knew everything that was going on. As kids or adults, we didn't get away with anything. I commented to my sister about how Momma would have enjoyed the internet, she could have found out anything she wanted to. My sister responded, at that time, Momma was the internet.

2 1/2 cups All Purpose Flour
3 teaspoons Baking Powder
1/4 teaspoon Salt
3/4 cup Butter or Margarine, softened
1 1/4 cups Sugar
3 Eggs
1 teaspoon Vanilla
1 cup Milk

1. Preheat oven to 350 degrees.
2. Grease and flour 2 - 9 inch round cake pans.
3. Sift Flour, Baking Powder, and Salt together. Set aside.
4. Cream Butter or Margarine until light.
5. Add Sugar to Butter or Margarine and cream until light and fluffy.
6. Add Eggs one at a time and mix until well blended.
7. Add Vanilla and mix until combined.
8. Add Flour mixture alternately with Milk. Do not over beat.
9. Divide mixture in half and place in prepared pans.
10. Bake 30-35 minutes or until a toothpick inserted into center comes out clean.
11. Let cool completely before icing.

Caramel Frosting

3 cups Sugar divided
3/4 cup Milk
1 Egg beaten
pinch of Salt
½ cup Butter softened (1 stick)

1. Sprinkle ½ cup Sugar in a heavy saucepan. Place over medium heat and cook stirring constantly until Sugar melts and syrup is light golden brown.
2. In another bowl, combine remaining 2 ½ cups Sugar, Milk, Beaten Egg and Salt mixing well, stir in Butter.
3. Stir Sugar mixture into hot caramelized sugar. The mixture will try to lump becoming smooth with further cooking. Cook over medium heat 15 to 20 minutes stirring frequently until mixture reaches thread stage (215 degrees on Candy Thermometer).
4. Cool 5 minutes, beat to almost spreading consistency and spread immediately on cool cake. Yield enough for one 2 layer cake.

Cherry Cobbler

This is more like Cherry Dumplings!

Dough:
1 recipe Momma Buttram's Biscuit Dough (Pages 71, 72)

Cherry Filling:
**14.5 ounce can of Red Tart Pitted Cherries - reserve juice in 2
   cup measuring cup**
1 cup Sugar
2 tablespoons Butter or Margarine melted
Water

1. Preheat oven to 375 degrees.
2. Grease a pan that you can use on top of the stove and in the oven. I used an 8 inch wide and 5 inch tall round enamel cast iron pan.
3. Prepare Biscuit Dough, divide in half.
4. Roll out half of dough or press with hands on a floured surface into a round circle that will fit in bottom of pan. Place in greased pan. Leave other half of Dough for top.
5. Drain juice from Cherries into a 2 cup measuring cup, add Water to measure 2 cups liquid.
6. Place drained Cherries in pan over the dough round and top with Cherry Juice/Water mixture, Sugar and Butter.
7. Make a round with remaining dough and place on top and cut several slits in dough with knife.
8. Bring mixture to boil and simmer 15 minutes.
9. Place pan in oven and bake 20 minutes until brown on top.

*Simmering on the top of the stove makes the inside dough like a dumpling and baking it makes the top brown and delicious.

Cherry O Cream Cheese Pie

It is a wonder anything got made around our house with Eagle Brand Milk in it. My sister, Margaret and I would eat it out of the can and what was left went in the pie.

Crust (or use a 6 ounce 9 inch prepared Graham Cracker Crust from the grocery store)
1 cup Graham Cracker Crumbs
3 tablespoons Sugar
3 tablespoons Butter, melted

1. Mix Graham Cracker Crumbs and Sugar together.
2. Stir melted Butter into mixture and press into a 9 inch pie pan. Set aside.

Graham Cracker Pie Crust
8 ounce package Cream Cheese
1 can Sweetened Condensed Milk
½ cup Lemon Juice
1 teaspoon Vanilla
1 can Cherry Pie Filling

1. Soften Cream Cheese to room temperature. Using an electric mixer, whip until fluffy.
2. Gradually add milk and beat until combined.
3. Beat in Lemon Juice and Vanilla.
4. Pour into Graham Cracker Crust.
5. Top with Cherry Pie Filling.
6. Keep refrigerated until serving time.

Georgia Mud Cake

This is a recipe from a dear friend Mary Peal. I practically grew up at her house when I was a teenager. She was a fantastic cook and I loved eating from her table. This was my favorite dessert, it was her take on a Mississippi Mud Cake.

2 sticks Butter or Margarine
2 cups Sugar
4 Eggs
1 1/2 cups All Purpose Flour
Dash of Salt
1/2 cup Cocoa
1/2 cup Peanuts
10 ounces Miniature Marshmallows

1. Preheat oven to 350 degrees.
2. Grease a 13 by 9 inch Baking Pan.
3. Cream Butter and Sugar together.
4. Add Eggs one at a time and blend well.
5. Sift Flour, Salt and Cocoa together and add to Egg mixture.
6. Fold in Nuts.
7. Bake 35 minutes until toothpick inserted comes out clean.
8. Remove cake from oven and pour Miniature Marshmallows on top of cake.
9. Set aside and start making the icing.

Icing

1/4 cup (1/2 stick) Butter or Margarine softened
1 box (16 ounces) Confectioners Sugar
1/2 cup Cocoa
1/2 cup Pet Milk (Evaporated Milk)
1 teaspoon Vanilla
1/2 cup Peanuts

1. Cream Butter or Margarine using an electric mixer.
2. Add Confectioners Sugar, Cocoa, Milk, and Vanilla and beat until

creamy.
3. Stir in Nuts.
4. Spread over cake.

*Mrs. Peal used Peanuts but you could use Pecans or Walnuts if you prefer.

Pam's Vegan Chocolate Cake

*Note - Make Filling first as it needs to be refrigerated 3-4 hours or overnight.

3 1/4 cups Whole Wheat Flour or Freshly Milled Soft White
   Wheat
2 teaspoons Baking Powder
2 teaspoons Baking Soda
1 teaspoon Salt
2/3 cup Cocoa
1 tablespoon Ener-G Egg Replacer mixed with 4 tablespoons
   Warm Water
1 cup Grape Seed Oil or Canola Oil
1 1/2 cups Sugar
3/4 cup Non-Dairy Milk
1 tablespoon Vanilla

1. Grease and flour 2 - 9 inch round cake pans.
2. Preheat Oven to 350 degrees.
3. Sift Flour three times, the last time add Baking Powder, Baking Soda, Salt, and Cocoa in large bowl. Be sure to put the wheat germ that remains in the sifter back in the flour so you won't lose any of the nutrients.
4. Mix Ener-G Egg Replacer with Water until creamy.
5. In a large electric mixer bowl mix Oil, Sugar, Non-Dairy Milk, and Vanilla.
6. Add Dry Ingredients and beat on low speed 1 minute.
7. Add Ener-G Egg Replacer mixture and beat on medium low speed 2 minutes.
8. Pour mixture into 2 - 9 inch round cake pans. Bake 25-30 minutes or until a toothpick inserted in center of each pan comes out clean.
9. Cool in pan for 10 minutes then turn out on a wire rack lined with kitchen towel.
10. Cool layers completely before icing.

Filling

1 cup Canned Coconut Milk (about 1/2 can)
1/8 teaspoon Salt
1 teaspoon Vanilla
1 1/2 cups Vegan Semi-Sweet Chocolate Chips
1/2 cup Vegan Mini Semi-Sweet Chocolate Chips

1. Shake Can of Coconut Milk and after opening stir until smooth.
2. Bring 1 cup (about 1/2 of can) Canned Coconut Milk to almost a boil over medium heat.
3. Reduce heat to low and add Salt, Vanilla and 1 1/2 cups Chocolate Chips.
4. Stir together until smooth.
5. Place chocolate mixture in refrigerator for 3-4 hours or overnight.
6. When mixture is cool and thick, fold in 1/2 cup Mini Chocolate Chips.
7. Place between layers of cooled chocolate cake.

Icing

1/2 cup (1 stick) Earth Balance Shortening (room temperature)
2 cups Vegan Powdered Sugar
1/4 cup Cocoa
2 teaspoons Vanilla
4-5 tablespoons Non-Dairy Milk (as needed)

1. Using electric mixer, cream Shortening.
2. Add Vegan Powdered Sugar, Cocoa and Vanilla and beat until smooth adding Non-Dairy Milk until desired spreading consistency.
3. When cake has cooled, place filling between layers and icing on top and sides of cake.

Chocolate Candy

Momma loved this chocolate candy. This recipe makes a lot of candy so give your extras away as Christmas gifts. Everyone loves to receive something homemade.

1 cup chopped Nuts
1 cup Coconut
1 ½ boxes Powdered Sugar
1 can Eagle Brand Milk (Sweetened Condensed Milk)
2 teaspoons Vanilla
1 stick Butter Melted

Coating

1 stick Paraffin Wax
16 ounces Chocolate Chips

1. In a bowl combine Nuts, Coconut and Powdered Sugar.
2. Add Eagle Brand Milk, Vanilla and Melted Butter and mix together.
3. Roll in small balls and place on a parchment or wax paper lined cookie sheet.
4. Put cookie sheets in freezer for 1 hour.
5. In double boiler put 1 stick Paraffin Wax and Chocolate Chips. Melt and dip cold candy into chocolate using a toothpick or a fork.

*Years ago we would use paraffin wax and chocolate chips but now you can buy chocolate formulated for dipping candies or use 2 tablespoons shortening to melt with 2 cups of chocolate chips instead of wax.

Lois Jordan's Chocolate Chip Cookies

When we visited my Aunt Lois she always made her Chocolate Chip Cookies for me because she knew that was the first thing I looked for when I walked in the house. When Momma and I made Chocolate Chip Cookies at home, we always used Lois' recipe.

3/4 cup Butter
½ cup Granulated Sugar
1 cup Brown Sugar, packed
1 teaspoon Vanilla
2 Eggs
2 cups All Purpose Flour (Lois added about 2 tablespoons more flour)
1 teaspoon Baking Soda
1 teaspoon Salt
2 cups (12 ounce package) Semi-Sweet Chocolate Chips
1 cup Pecans chopped

1. Preheat oven to 375 degrees.
2. Cream the Butter, Sugars and Vanilla until light and fluffy.
3. Add the Eggs and beat well.
4. Sift together the Flour, Baking Soda and Salt and add to the creamed mixture. Mix well.
5. Add the Chocolate Chips and Nuts and blend well.
6. Drop by teaspoonful onto lightly greased baking sheet.
7. Bake 8 to 10 minutes.

Chocolate Fudge Nut Pie

If you like Chocolate Fudge, you will love this pie. It is so creamy and the crunch of the nuts and coconut take it over the top.

1/2 stick Butter or Margarine melted
2 Eggs
5 ounces Pet Milk (Evaporated Milk)
1 1/2 cups Sugar
4 tablespoons Cocoa
1 teaspoon Vanilla
1 cup Pecans or 1/2 cup Pecans and 1/2 cup Coconut
1 unbaked Pie Crust

1. Preheat oven to 310.
2. Prepare Pie Crust.
3. Melt Butter or Margarine and set aside.
4. Using an electric mixer, beat Eggs together.
5. Add Milk to Eggs and beat.
6. Beat in Melted Butter or Margarine.
7. Add Sugar, Cocoa and Vanilla into Egg mixture and beat until combined.
8. Stir in Pecans and Coconut if using.
9. Pour into Pie Crust and bake 1 hour.

*The low oven temperature enables the pie to cook evenly and the edges don't get done before the middle of the pie.

Chocolate Pound Cake

1/2 cup Butter
1/2 cup Crisco
3 cups Sugar
5 Eggs
1 teaspoon Vanilla
3 cups Plain All Purpose Flour
1/4 teaspoon Salt
3/4 teaspoon Baking Powder
1/2 cup Cocoa
1 1/4 cups Sweet Milk

1. Preheat oven to 300 degrees.
2. Grease and flour a tube pan.
3. Using an electric mixer, cream Butter and Crisco together.
4. To creamed mixture add Sugar and continue to beat until light and fluffy.
5. Add Eggs one at a time until incorporated.
6. Add Vanilla and beat on low until everything is mixed together.
7. Sift Flour, Salt, Baking Powder and Cocoa together.
8. Add Flour mixture alternately with Milk just until everything is mixed together. Do not over beat.
9. Pour batter into prepared tube pan.
10. Bake 1 hour and 25 minutes until a toothpick inserted comes out clean.
11. Let cool in pan 10 minutes before turning out.

Icing

2 cups Sugar
1/4 cup Cocoa
1/4 teaspoon Salt
2/3 cup Milk
1/2 cup Shortening

1. In a saucepan, mix Sugar, Cocoa and Salt together.

2. Stir in Milk.
3. Add Shortening.
4. Boil 2 minutes.
5. Pour over cooled cake.

Chocolate Pie

I remember coming home from school and Momma would have a pie on the table and I knew it was either Chocolate or Coconut. I would examine the pie carefully because it was a game to me...trying to figure out which it was. It didn't matter, they were both wonderful.

1 cup Sugar
3 tablespoons All Purpose Flour
3 tablespoons Cocoa
3 Egg Yolks
12 ounce Can Evaporated Milk
1 tablespoon Vanilla
1 baked pie shell (Momma used Ritz Deep Dish, I like Pillsbury found in the refrigerator section or homemade crust is always best.)

1. Preheat oven to 350 degrees.
2. Prepare and bake your Pie Crust according to directions.
3. In a double boiler stir together Sugar, Flour and Cocoa.
4. Add Egg Yolks and stir together.
5. Carefully stir in Evaporated Milk.
6. Cook and stir in double boiler until thick.
7. Remove from heat and add Vanilla. Pour into baked Pie Shell.
8. Beat 3 Egg Whites until stiff peaks form then add 3 tablespoons Sugar.
9. Place beaten Egg Whites on top of pie and bake in 350 degree oven about 15 minutes or until brown.

Christmas Cake

This recipe is from Momma's sister, Murray Opal Crowder. She died in the early 70's. She was a fabulous cook. I remember eating the best meat loaf I ever had at her house. She served it with a tomato sauce. I wish I had that recipe!

1 cup Butter
2 cups Sugar
3 Eggs
1 cup Blackberry Jam
1 cup chopped Nuts
1 cup glazed Cherries
1 cup glazed Pineapple or Raisins
1 cup mashed Potato
1 ½ cups Coconut
1 teaspoon Allspice
2/3 cup Buttermilk
1 teaspoon Vanilla flavoring
1 ½ cups sifted Cake Flour
1 ½ cups sifted All Purpose Flour
1 teaspoon Soda
pinch Salt

1. Preheat oven to 250 degrees.
2. Cream Butter and Sugar together and then add Eggs one at a time, beating well after each.
3. Add Jam, Nuts, Cherries, Pineapple or Raisins, Potatoes, Coconut and Allspice.
4. Stir in Buttermilk, then Vanilla.
5. Sift Flour with Soda and Salt and fold into batter until smooth.
6. Bake in 2 or 3 layers at 250 degrees for about 1 ½ hours or until done.

Pineapple Filling

3 tablespoons Flour
1 cup Sugar
1/4 teaspoon Salt

1 ½ cups Pineapple Juice
½ stick Oleo (Margarine)
3 Egg Yolks
1 can (20 ounce) Crushed Pineapple (drained)
1 tsp. Vanilla

1. Place Pineapple Juice in a Saucepan.
2. Mix Flour, Sugar and Salt and stir into Pineapple Juice.
3. Add Oleo and cook over low heat until Oleo is melted.
4. Add beaten Egg Yolks.
5. Cook until thick, stirring constantly, add Crushed Pineapple.
6. Remove from heat. Add Vanilla.
7. Spread between and on top of layers.

Coconut Pie

This is the same recipe as the Chocolate Pie but you add coconut instead. Absolutely delicious!

1 cup Sugar
3 tablespoons All Purpose Flour
3 Egg Yolks
12 ounce Can Evaporated Milk
3.5 ounce can Angel Flake Coconut
1 tablespoon Vanilla
1 baked pie shell (Momma used Ritz Deep Dish, I like Pillsbury found in the refrigerator section or homemade crust is always best.)

1. Preheat oven to 350 degrees.
2. Prepare and bake your Pie Crust according to directions.
3. In a double boiler stir together Sugar and Flour.
4. Add Egg Yolks and stir together.
5. Carefully stir in Evaporated Milk.
6. Cook and stir in double boiler until thick.
7. Add Coconut and stir well.
8. Remove from heat and add Vanilla. Pour into baked Pie Shell.
9. Beat 3 Egg Whites until stiff peaks form then add 3 tablespoons Sugar.
10. Place beaten Egg Whites on top of pie and bake in 350 degree oven about 15 minutes or until brown.

The Hudson Cream Cheese Pound Cake

Billy's Mama made this cake for him when he was young. Momma Buttram would have loved this. If I ever make this cake for anyone, they expect it when I visit or they come to our house. We had this for our wedding cake with Strawberries and Whipped Cream. It is so famous we call it 'The Hudson Cream Cheese Pound Cake'.

2 sticks Butter, room temperature
1 stick Margarine, room temperature
8 ounce package Cream Cheese, room temperature
3 cups Sugar
6 Eggs, room temperature
1 teaspoon Vanilla
1 teaspoon Almond Extract
3 cups Cake Flour

1. Preheat oven to 250 degrees. Grease and flour a tube pan.
2. Put a small pan of water on bottom shelf of oven, this will prevent cake from drying out.
3. Using an electric mixer, cream Butter, Margarine and Cream Cheese until light and fluffy.
4. Add Sugar and beat until combined and light.
5. Add Eggs one at a time and mix well.
6. Add Vanilla and Almond Extract and mix well.
7. Gradually add Flour and mix just until combined. Don't over mix.
8. Place batter in a tube pan and cook at 250 for 1 hour then raise oven temperature to 300 and bake 1 hour longer.
9. Leave in pan for 15 minutes before turning out.

*This cake freezes well.

Date Nut Roll

My sister's favorite Christmas treat was the Date Nut Roll and reading the recipe I know why. It starts with HOMEMADE Eagle Brand Milk!! I'll never forget seeing the candy roll wrapped in an old dish towel cooling on the counter.

2 cups Sugar
12 ounce can Evaporated Milk
1 cup chopped Dates
1 cup chopped Nuts
1 teaspoon Vanilla

1. In a 2 quart saucepan, combine Sugar and Evaporated Milk.
2. Cook stirring occasionally until a few drops form a soft ball in cold water. (235 degrees on a Candy Thermometer)
3. Add 1 cup Chopped Dates and continue cooking until a drop forms a hard ball in cold water. (250 degrees on a Candy Thermometer)
4. Remove from heat and add 1 cup Chopped Nuts and 1 teaspoon Vanilla.
5. Cool at room temperature until lukewarm or until the hand can be placed on the bottom of the pan.
6. Beat until stiff enough to knead into a roll and wrap in a cloth.
7. Remove the cloth when firm and cut into ½ inch slices. Makes about 3 dozen slices.

Divinity Candy

Divinity Candy was always on Momma's Beautiful Crystal Lazy Susan Tray at Christmas along with Chocolate Fudge, Date Nut Roll, Salted Nuts, Orange Slice Candy, Vanilla Cream Dark Chocolate Drops and Chocolate Covered Cherries. Momma made the Divinity especially for my brother, Duran.

2 cups Sugar
1/4 cup Water
1/2 cup White Corn Syrup
1 teaspoon Vanilla
2 Egg Whites
1 cup Chopped Pecans or Walnuts if desired

1. Place Sugar, Water and Corn Syrup in a saucepan and bring to a boil.
2. Reduce heat and let cook until mixture forms a hard ball (250 degrees).
3. Beat Egg Whites with wire wisk of electric mixer until stiff peaks form.
4. Pour sugar mixture slowly over Egg Whites in mixer and beat gently.
Add Vanilla and beat until it loses its gloss.
5. Stir in food color and chopped Nuts if desired.
6. Drop onto wax paper lined baking sheet and let sit until cool and set.
7. Store in an air tight container at room temperature.

*Momma added green food coloring to make it festive.

Japanese Fruit Cake

Another Christmas Cake Momma made every year was the Japanese Fruit Cake. I especially loved the cake batter with all of the spices, raisins and nuts and was eager to lick the bowl.

1 cup Butter
2 cups Sugar
4 Eggs
3 cups All Purpose Flour
½ teaspoon Salt
1 teaspoon Soda
1 cup Buttermilk
1 cup chopped Raisins*
1 cup chopped Pecans or Walnuts
1 teaspoon Cinnamon
1 teaspoon Allspice
1 teaspoon Cloves
1 teaspoon Nutmeg

1. Preheat oven to 350 degrees.
2. Grease and flour 3 - 9 inch round cake pans.
3. Using an electric mixer, cream Butter and Sugar together until light and fluffy.
4. Add Eggs one at a time beating well between each Egg.
5. Sift Flour, Salt and Soda together.
6. Add Flour Mixture to creamed mixture alternately with Buttermilk.
7. Pour 2/3 of mixture into two greased and floured pans.
8. Place raisins and nuts in a small bowl and dust with a little flour.
9. Stir Raisins, Nuts, Cinnamon, Allspice, Cloves and Nutmeg into remaining batter. Pour into cake pan.
10. Bake cake layers 25-30 minutes until a toothpick inserted in center comes out clean.

Filling

2 ½ cups Sugar
2 Tablespoons All Purpose Flour

2 Lemons - Juice and grated Lemon Peel from both
2 packages Frozen Coconut (Momma always used 1 fresh
** coconut)**
1 ½ cups Hot Water

1. Mix Sugar and Flour together in a 2 quart saucepan.
2. Add Lemon Juice and Lemon Peel.
3. Stir in Coconut and Hot Water and cook until thick.
4. Spread between layers and over top and sides of cake. (Punch holes in cake with toothpick before icing so that icing will go into cake layer, this is a thin icing). The spice layer should be in the middle.

*Soak raisins in hot water 5 minutes and drain before chopping.

Fruit Pie

1 cup Sugar
2 Eggs
1/2 stick Butter melted (1/4 cup)
1 teaspoon Vanilla
1 tablespoon Vinegar
1/2 cup Chopped Nuts
1/2 cup Raisins
1/2 cup Angel Flake Coconut
Unbaked Pie Shell

1. Preheat Oven to 300 degrees.
2. Prepare Pie Shell.
3. Mix Sugar, Eggs, melted Butter, Vanilla and Vinegar together.
4. Stir in Nuts, Raisins, Coconut and mix well.
5. Pour into Pie Shell.
6. Bake 50 to 60 minutes.

Fudge Candy

I love this Fudge recipe. It is so good and simple. This was always on Momma's Christmas tray with Divinity Candy and the Date Nut Roll. This is probably the first recipe I learned to make.

3 cups Sugar
2/3 cup Cocoa
1/8 teaspoon Salt
1 1/2 cups Milk (or use 1 can evaporated milk and add enough
   water to make 1 1/2 cups)
4 tablespoons Butter or Margarine
1 teaspoon Vanilla
1 cup chopped Pecans or Walnuts optional

1. Grease an 8x8 inch pan or Pyrex dish.
2. Place Sugar, Cocoa and Salt in saucepan. I prefer to use a cast iron skillet. Stir Sugar, Cocoa and Salt together.
3. Add Milk and stir to blend the Sugar mixture into the milk.
4. Cook until mixture reaches 238 degrees on a candy thermometer or until a little of mixture dropped into cold water forms a soft ball.
5. Remove from heat and add Butter or Margarine and Vanilla.
6. Beat with a wooden spoon until the fudge loses its sheen.
7. Stir in Nuts if desired.
8. Pour into prepared pan and let cool.

Fudge Pie

We had a bakery in our area that was famous for these pies. My sister found the recipe in an old Cookbook from Alabama and the pie tastes just like the ones from the bakery.

2 Eggs
1/2 stick Butter Melted (1/4 cup)
3 1/2 tablespoons Cocoa
1 small can Evaporated Milk (5 ounces)
1 1/2 cups Sugar
1 teaspoon Vanilla
1 unbaked Pie Shell

1. Preheat oven to 350 degrees.
2. In a blender blend the eggs.
3. Mix Melted Butter and Cocoa together in separate bowl adding a little of the milk and blend until smooth.
4. Put Butter Cocoa mixture in blender and blend with eggs.
5. Add remaining Milk to blender and blend well.
6. Add Sugar and Vanilla to blender and blend well.
7. Pour into unbaked pie shell.
8. Bake 30 minutes at 350 or until center just jiggles but not soupy.

*You can use a hand held mixer instead of a blender. The blender just makes a smoother and creamier consistency.

Italian Cream Cake

I made this cake for my sweet husband when we were dating, needless to say, I made a good impression.

5 Eggs separated
2 cups All Purpose Flour
1 teaspoon Baking Soda
1/2 cup (1 stick) Butter or Margarine
1/2 cup Shortening
2 cups Sugar
1 cup Buttermilk
1 teaspoon Vanilla
1 small can (3.5 ounces) Angel Flake Coconut
1 cup Pecans chopped

1. Preheat oven to 350 degrees.
2. Grease and flour 3 - 9 inch round cake pans.
3. Beat 5 Egg Whites until stiff peaks form and set aside.
4. Sift Flour and Baking Soda together and set aside.
5. Cream Butter or Margarine and Shortening.
6. Add Sugar to Butter mixture and cream until light and fluffy.
7. Add 5 Egg Yolks and mix well.
8. Add Flour mixture alternately with Buttermilk, beginning and ending with dry ingredients.
9. Add Vanilla, Coconut and Nuts.
10. Fold in stiffly beaten Egg Whites.
11. Pour into cake pans and bake 30-35 minutes until a toothpick inserted into the center comes out clean.

Icing

1/4 cup Butter or Margarine softened (1/2 stick)
8 ounce package Cream Cheese
1 pound box Confectioners Sugar
1 teaspoon Vanilla
Milk as needed

1 cup Pecans chopped (optional)

1. Cream Butter or Margarine and Cream Cheese together.
2. Add Confectioners Sugar and Vanilla and mix well.
3. If mixture is too stiff, add milk 1 teaspoon at a time until desired consistency.
4. Stir in Pecans if using.
5. Place between cake layers and on top and sides of cooled cake.

Pam's Vegan Italian Cream Cake

I formulated this recipe because I like to bake with Freshly Milled Flour, No Eggs or Butter.

3 ¾ cups Whole Wheat Flour or Freshly Milled Soft White Wheat
2 teaspoons Baking Powder
2 teaspoons Baking Soda
1 teaspoon Salt
1 1/2 cups Sugar or Sugar in the Raw
¾ cup Grape Seed Oil or Canola Oil
1 cup Non-Dairy Milk
2 teaspoons Vanilla
1 cup Chopped Walnuts or Pecans
1 cup Bakers Angel Flake Sweetened Coconut

1. Grease and flour 2 - 9 inch round cake pans.
2. Preheat Oven to 350 degrees.
3. Chop Pecans.
4. Sift Flour three times, the last time add Baking Powder, Baking Soda, and Salt, in large bowl. Be sure to put the wheat germ that remains in the sifter back in the flour so you won't lose any of the nutrients.
5. Stir Sugar into Flour mixture.
6. In a separate bowl, wisk Oil, Non-Dairy Milk, and Vanilla.
7. Pour wet mixture over dry mixture and wisk together well. Fold in Nuts and Coconut.
8. Pour mixture into 2 - 9 inch round cake pans. Bake 25-30 minutes or until a toothpick inserted in center of each pan comes out clean.
9. Cool in pan for 10 minutes then turn out on a wire rack lined with kitchen towel.
10. Cool layers completely before icing.

Icing

1/2 cup (1 stick) Earth Balance Vegan Buttery Stick (room temperature)
8 ounce container Soy Cream Cheese (room temperature)

3 cups Vegan Powdered Sugar
1 teaspoon Vanilla
1-2 tablespoons Non-Dairy Milk (if needed)
1 cup Chopped Walnuts or Pecans

1. Using electric mixer, cream Buttery Stick and Soy Cream Cheese.
2. Add Vegan Powdered Sugar and Vanilla and beat until smooth. (Add Non-Dairy Milk if needed).
3. Stir in Chopped Nuts.
4. When cake has cooled, place icing between layers and on top and sides of cake.

The "Lane Cake"

Momma was a master at cake baking and she taught me how to make cakes starting with the hardest – her "Christmas" cakes. We always made cakes from scratch. I remember buying my first cake mix. I was so embarrassed, I hid it in the buggy under the groceries and was afraid someone I knew would see me in the check-out lane.

This is the most beautiful cake you can make. This tall four layer cake looks like it is encrusted with jewels. This was mine and Daddy's favorite Christmas Cake. I am so glad Momma taught me how to make it.

The recipe is written in a very old fashioned way. I gave a copy to my friend, Sharon Schleyer and this is the thank you note she sent back:

Pam,

Thank you so much for this recipe. Just reading it brings back some really special memories I have of my Mom and GrandMomma. I can picture that old wood cooking stove, the creek and the mountain behind the house at McKinsey Creek where I played. I tried to retype this so I would be able to print and make copies for my babies when they get old enough to go through my cookbook. I can only hope that they will realize the treasure it is.

Sharon

The Recipe:
First read through the entire recipe. These are the ingredients needed for cake and frosting. Make no substitutions. All measurements are level. Assemble ingredients, and let stand at room temperature 1 hour.

CAKE LAYERS
1 cup Butter
2 cups Granulated Sugar
1 teaspoon Vanilla
3 1/4 cups sifted All-Purpose Flour
3 ½ teaspoons Double Acting Baking Powder
3/4 teaspoon Salt
1 cup Milk
8 Egg Whites

FROSTING
12 Egg Yolks
1 3/4 cups Granulated Sugar
½ teaspoon Salt
3/4 cup Butter or Margarine
½ cup Rye or Bourbon Whiskey
1 ½ cups course chopped Pecans
1 ½ cups chopped seedless Raisins
1 ½ cups shredded fresh Coconut
1 ½ cups quartered Candied Cherries

TO MAKE THE LAYERS

1. Use four round 9 inch layer pans, 1 inch deep; grease pans with a little butter and line bottoms with waxed paper cut to fit. (If you have only 2 pans, let the batter stand while baking 2 layers. After removing first 2 baked layers, wash and dry pans. Grease and line bottom of pans.

2. Turn on oven set at 375 degrees. If oven has no control, use a portable oven thermometer and keep correct temperature by controlling heat.

3. With an electric mixer or a large spoon, beat 1 cup butter in large bowl until fluffy.

4. Gradually add 2 cups sugar, and beat after each addition until fluffy.

5. Add 1 teaspoon vanilla, and beat until mixture is as light as whipped cream.

6. Sift, then lightly spoon flour into measuring cup. Level top with spatula. Put 3 1/4 cups measured sifted flour into sifter. (Do not use cake flour or self-rising flour).

7. Add 3 ½ teaspoons double acting baking powder and 3/4 teaspoons salt. Sift flour, baking powder and salt into a large piece of waxed paper.

8. To butter mixture, add flour mixture, alternately with 1 cup milk in small amounts beating each time.

9. Thoroughly wash and dry electric mixer or rotary beater. (Even a speck of butter on the beater will prevent egg whites from becoming stiff). Beat 8 egg whites until they stand in soft glossy points, but not until dry. (Meanwhile cover yolks).

10. With a large spoon gently fold whites into batter. To do this, drop beaten whites on top of batter. With side of spoon, cut down through batter to bottom of bowl. Turn spoon and bring it up alongside of bowl, folding some batter over whites. Do not push down on whites. Continue until whites are evenly distributed.

11. Divide batter evenly among 4 pans, and spread to sides with spatula. (If you have only 2 pans, see step 1.)

12. Have top rack about middle of oven. Put second rack about 2 inches below. Place pans two pans on each rack so that one pan is set directly beneath another. Surface springs back when done. (Check after 15 minutes of cooking since layers are thin.)

13. Put pans on cake racks for 5 minutes. Carefully loosen around edges with spatula. Turn layers upside down on rack. Slowly peel off paper. Cool before frosting.

TO MAKE THE FROSTING

1. Prepare fruits and nuts.

2. Put 12 egg yolks in top part of double boiler, and beat slightly with rotary beater.

3. Add 1 3/4 cups sugar, ½ teaspoon salt and 3/4 cup butter.

4. Cook over simmering water, stirring constantly until sugar is dissolved, butter melts and mixture is slightly thickened. Do not overcook or let egg yolks become scrambled in appearance. Mixture should be almost translucent.

5. Remove from heat and add ½ cup rye or bourbon.

6. Beat mixture 1 minute with rotary beater. Add 1 ½ cups chopped pecans, 1 ½ cups chopped seedless raisins, 1 ½ cups shredded fresh coconut and 1 ½ cups quartered candied cherries. If double boiler is too small to hold all of this, mix all ingredients in a large bowl. Cool.

TO FROST CAKE AND STORE

1. Spread frosting between layers and on top and side. After an hour, if any has dripped off on plate, use a spatula to spread it back on sides. Repeat if necessary.

2. Cover with cake cover or loosely with foil and store to ripen several days in a cool place. Stored this way, cake will keep well for several weeks. If frozen, then wrap in vapor proof wrapping, stored in freezer will keep indefinitely.

Lemon Icebox Pie

Momma always made this pie at least once a month. Her Lemon Icebox Pie was the old fashioned one that you didn't bake that is why it was called Lemon Icebox. I've included a recipe that bakes the filling in the stove if you are afraid of raw eggs. She used Vanilla Wafers for her crust and put wafers around the edge of the pie plate so every piece of pie had one or two Vanilla Wafer Cookies. That was the prize for eating your piece of pie.

Crust:
1 1/2 cups Crushed Vanilla Wafers
1/3 cup Butter melted

1. Combine Crushed Vanilla Wafers and melted Butter together. Press into a 9 inch pie plate.
2. Line outside of pie pan with Vanilla Wafers so that they stand up against the side of the pan. Set aside.

Filling:
2 Egg Yolks
1/2 cup Freshly Squeezed Lemon Juice
14 ounce can Eagle Brand Milk (Sweetened Condensed Milk)

1. Beat Egg Yolks in a bowl with electric mixer.
2. Beat in Lemon Juice.
3. Add Eagle Brand Milk and beat until combined.
4. Pour into prepared pie shell and refrigerate until completely chilled.
5. Serve with Whip Cream if desired.

Pam's Lemon Pie

This is my take on a Lemon Icebox Pie. The filling is baked in the oven and topped with meringue.

Crust (or use a 6 ounce 9 inch prepared Graham Cracker Crust from the grocery store)
1 cup Graham Cracker Crumbs
3 tablespoons Sugar
3 tablespoons Butter, melted

1. Mix Graham Cracker Crumbs and Sugar together.
2. Stir melted Butter into mixture and press into a 9 inch pie pan. Set aside.

Filling
3 Egg Yolks
1/2 cup Lemon Juice
14 ounce can Eagle Brand Milk (Sweetened Condensed Milk)
3 Egg Whites
5 tablespoons Sugar
1/4 teaspoon Cream of Tartar

1. Preheat Oven to 325 degrees.
2. Beat Egg Yolks in a bowl of an electric mixer.
3. Beat in Lemon Juice.
4. Add Eagle Brand Milk and mix until combined.
5. Pour into prepared Pie Shell.
6. Bake 20 minutes.
7. After pie has been baking 15 minutes, start Meringue.
8. Put Egg Whites in a bowl of an electric mixer and beat until foamy.
9. Add Sugar and Cream of Tartar and beat until stiff peaks form.
10. Remove Pie from oven and top with Meringue spreading to edges.
11. Return pie to oven and bake 10 minutes or until Meringue is golden brown.
12. Let pie cool and place in refrigerator.
13. Serve chilled.

*If you do not want to put Meringue on the pie, bake pie 25 minutes and let cool and refrigerate until cold and serve with Whip Cream.

Maple Pecan Pralines

3 cups Sugar
1 cup Evaporated Milk
2/3 cup Light Corn Syrup
2 tablespoons Butter or Margarine
1/4 teaspoon Cream of Tartar
2 cups Pecan Pieces
2 teaspoons Maple Flavoring

1. Combine Sugar, Milk, Corn Syrup, Butter and Cream of Tartar in a Dutch oven and heat to boiling stirring constantly.
2. Stir in Pecan Pieces, cook over medium heat stirring occasionally until mixture reaches a soft ball stage (235 degrees).
3. Remove from heat, stir in Maple Flavoring.
4. Beat with a wooden spoon 5 to 8 minutes or until the mixture is creamy and begins to thicken.
5. Working rapidly, drop by rounded tablespoonful onto waxed paper. Let cool.
6. Yield 2 dozen.

Mardi Gras Cake

2/3 cup Butterscotch Morsels
1/4 cup Water
2 1/4 cups All Purpose Flour
1 teaspoon Salt
1 teaspoon Baking Soda
1/4 teaspoon Baking Powder
1 1/4 cups Sugar
1/2 cup Butter or Margarine
3 Eggs
1 cup Buttermilk

1. Preheat oven to 375 degrees.
2. Grease and Flour 2 - 9 inch round cake pans.
3. Melt Butterscotch Morsels with Water in a saucepan.
4. Sift Flour, Salt, Baking Soda, and Baking Powder. Set aside.
5. Using an electric mixer, cream Butter or Margarine and add Sugar and beat until light and fluffy.
6. Add Eggs to Sugar mixture beating well after each addition.
7. Stir in melted Butterscotch Morsels and mix well.
8. Add dry ingredients alternately with Buttermilk. Don't over beat.
9. Divide batter evenly into 2 - 9 inch cake pans.
10. Bake 25-30 minutes or until a toothpick inserted comes out clean.
11. Cool completely, then spread filling between layers and ice with frosting.

Filling

1 cup Sugar
2 tablespoons Cornstarch
1 cup Evaporated Milk
2/3 cup Water
2/3 cup Butterscotch Morsels
2 beaten Egg Yolks (reserve Egg Whites for Icing)
2 tablespoons Butter
2 cups Angel Flake Coconut

2 cups Nuts

1. In a 2 quart saucepan, combine Sugar and Cornstarch.
2. Add Milk, Water, Butterscotch Morsels, and Egg Yolks.
3. Cook over medium heat, stirring constantly until thick.
4. Remove from heat, add Butter, Coconut and Nuts.
5. Place cake layer on a plate and top with 1/2 of filling.
6. Place remaining layer on cake and top with remaining filling.

Icing

1/2 cup Sugar
2 tablespoons Water
1/4 cup Light Corn Syrup
2 Egg Whites
1 teaspoon Vanilla

1. Mix Sugar, Water and Corn Syrup in a saucepan.
2. Cover pan and bring to a boil.
3. Remove cover and let mixture cook until syrup spins a 6 to 8 inch thread (215 degrees on a candy thermometer).
4. Just before syrup is ready, beat Egg Whites until stiff enough to hold a point.
5. Pour hot syrup very slowly in a thin stream into the beaten Egg Whites and continue beating until frosting holds peaks.
6. Blend in Vanilla.
7. Spread Icing around sides of cake.

Old Fashioned Dark Fruit Cake

I usually make the Fruit Cake before Thanksgiving so that it can "ripen". People who make fun of Fruit Cake have never spent hours making them and enjoyed the wonderful taste of the candied fruit ripened with the taste of wine or whiskey.

Now days, I have it easy, the nuts are shelled and most of the fruit is cut up. I remember all of us sitting around the table cracking nuts and cutting up fruit which took more than the couple of hours it takes me to assemble this cake. Making this cake was an all-day affair then but it was fun and the memories of sitting at the kitchen table with my Momma and Daddy preparing nuts and fruit for a Fruit Cake is so precious.

½ pound Butter (2 sticks softened)
3 cups Dark Brown Sugar
6 Eggs separated
1 tablespoon Cinnamon
1 tablespoon Allspice
½ cup Molasses
½ cup Sour Milk (Buttermilk)
4 cups All Purpose Flour
1 teaspoon Baking Soda - dissolved in a few tablespoons water
1 pack Seedless Raisins (1 250 gram box)
1 pound English Walnuts (2 cups Walnuts or Pecans)
32 ounce pack of Candied Fruit Cake Mix*
1 package Dates (8 ounce package Pitted Dates)

1. Preheat oven to 275 degrees.
2. Separate Eggs and beat Egg Whites until stiff peaks form. Set aside.
3. Using an electric mixer and large bowl, cream Butter and Sugar together until light and fluffy.
4. Add beaten Egg Yolks and beat until incorporated and fluffy.
5. Add the Cinnamon, Allspice, Molasses and Sour Milk. Beat together well.
6. Add the Flour and beat just until mixed together.
7. Fold in the stiffly beaten egg whites.
8. Add the soda that has been dissolved in a few tablespoons of water.

9.   Put the fruit and nuts in a very large bowl and dust with a few tablespoons of flour.

10. Pour the batter over the fruit and mix together.

11. This will make several cakes depending on size of the pans you choose. You can make small cakes to give away or use two large tube pans. Make sure you have greased and floured any pan you use.

12. Bake 4 to 5 hours 275 degrees depending on how large your pan is. Make sure you check your cakes as you probably won't cook this long unless your pan is large. A toothpick inserted into center should come out clean. (Small pans may only take 1 hour to cook.)

13. Momma used to pour wine over her fruit cakes but Billy and I put them in large Tupperware cake containers and put a shot glass of whisky in the container and sliced apples on top of cake. Sometimes we just pour the whisky over the cakes. Let the cake sit a week or more to ripen in a cool place.

*I usually buy what I find at the grocery store for the Candied Fruit. Sometimes I buy the large pack of mixed Candied Fruit or I may buy a couple of small containers of red and green cherries and smaller containers of the fruit cake mix.

Fruit Cake

Billy's Momma was a great baker. Here is Mrs. Hudson's version of a Fruit Cake.

1 cup Butter
1 cup Sugar
5 large Eggs (separated)
1/2 cup Orange Juice
1 glass Grape Jelly (probably a cup)
2 1/2 cups all Purpose Flour plus 1/2 cup for Fruit and Nuts
1 teaspoon Baking Powder
1 teaspoon Cinnamon
1/2 teaspoon Nutmeg
1/2 teaspoon Allspice
1/2 teaspoon Cloves
1 pound Candied Cherries
1 pound Candied Pineapple
1 pound Pecans
1 pound Golden Raisins
1/2 pound Almonds
1/4 pound Candied Citron
1/8 pound Candied Lemon Peel
1/8 pound Candied Orange Peel
3.5 ounce can Angel Flake Coconut

1. Preheat oven to 250 degrees.
2. Grease and Flour a Tube Pan.
3. Cut up Candied Fruits and Nuts if needed and sprinkle with 1/2 cup Flour and mix well.
4. Sift Flour, Baking Powder, Cinnamon, Nutmeg, Allspice, and Cloves together. Set aside.
5. Beat Egg Whites until stiff Peaks form and set aside.
6. Cream Butter and Sugar together until light and fluffy.
7. Add Egg Yolks and mix well.
8. Beat in Flour mixture, Orange Juice and Grape Jelly.
9. Fold in Beaten Egg Whites.
10. Add Fruit, Nuts and Coconut.

11. Pour into a large tube pan.
12. Bake 2 1/2 to 3 hours.

Orange Pecan Pie

3 Eggs Beaten
1/2 cup Sugar
1 cup Dark Karo Syrup
1 tablespoon Grated Orange Rind
1/3 cup Orange Juice
1 tablespoon All Purpose Flour
1/4 teaspoon Salt
1 cup Chopped Pecans
1 unbaked 9 inch Pie Shell
1/4 cup Pecan Halves

1. Preheat oven to 350 degrees.
2. Prepare Pie Shell
3. Combine Eggs, Sugar, Syrup, Orange Rind, Orange Juice, Flour and Salt and beat at medium speed of electric mixer until blended well.
4. Stir in Chopped Pecans.
5. Pour mixture into pie shell.
6. Arrange pecan halves over top.
7. Bake 55 to 60 minutes.

*I love to add 1/4 cup Bourbon to my Pecan Pies so in this case, I think an addition of 2 to 4 tablespoons of Grand Marnier would be appropriate.

Peach Cobbler

I remember Momma made this at least once a month, it was so easy to whip up. I think every Southern Belle has this in her recipe box.

1 stick Butter (1/2 cup)
1/2 cup All Purpose Flour
1 cup Sugar
1 cup Milk
15 ounce can Peaches undrained
Optional 1 teaspoon Vanilla and 3/4 teaspoon Cinnamon

1. Preheat oven to 375 degrees.
2. Place Butter in 9 inch pan or a 1 quart Pyrex dish and put in oven to melt.
3. In a bowl mix Flour and Sugar, then gradually add Milk. Mix well. If desired, add Vanilla and Cinnamon at this time.
4. Pour mixture in pan with butter.
5. Pour can of undrained Peaches over, do not mix.
6. Bake 375 until done, about 30 minutes. (You can tell it is done when the top browns.)

*My brother and his wife use this recipe for their Cherry Pie. They substitute Comstock Cherry Pie Filling for the Peaches.

Peach Pies

3 cups sliced Fresh or Frozen Peaches thawed
3/4 cup Sugar
3-4 tablespoons Water
1 recipe of Momma Buttram's Biscuits (Pages 71, 72)
1/4 cup melted Butter or Margarine

1. Peel and slice Peaches if using fresh. If using frozen sliced Peaches thaw.
2. Place Peaches, Sugar and Water in a saucepan.
3. Bring Peaches to a boil and cover and simmer on low heat 15 minutes.
4. Remove cover from Peaches and mash with a potato masher until peaches are chunky. Simmer Peaches 10 minutes longer.
5. Set aside to cool completely.
6. Preheat oven to 375 degrees and spray a baking sheet with cooking spray.
7. Prepare Biscuit Recipe.
8. Make 8 equal balls with Biscuit dough.
9. On a floured surface, roll each ball into a 5 inch round.
10. Place 1 ½ to 2 tablespoons of the Peach mixture on one side of the dough and fold remaining dough over, it will look like a half moon.
11. Crimp edges of dough with a fork to keep pie closed.
12. Place on baking sheet and continue making pies.
13. Using a fork punch tops of pies three times to vent.
14. Spoon melted Butter or Margarine over each pie.
15. Bake 20-25 minutes until golden brown.

Pecan Pie

Momma used this recipe that she found on the Karo Syrup jar. She used the Light Karo Syrup.

1 cup Light Karo Corn Syrup
3 Eggs
1 cup Sugar
2 tablespoons Butter melted
1 teaspoon Vanilla
1 to 1 1/2 cups Pecan Halves
1 unbaked Pie Shell

1. Preheat oven to 350 degrees.
2. Prepare Pie Shell.
3. In a mixing bowl, combine Corn Syrup, Eggs, Sugar, Butter and Vanilla.
4. Stir in Pecans. Pour into Pie Shell.
5. Bake 60 to 70 minutes.
6. Cool for 2 hours before cutting.
7. Store in refrigerator.

*This pie freezes well. I usually make several ahead for Christmas Parties.
**To make Bourbon Pecan Pie, add 1/4 cup Bourbon before stirring in the Pecans.

Pinto Bean Pie

I remember the first time Momma made this pie. I said, "Pinto Bean Pie, yuck"! But 'Boy, Hidy!' it was great and she made it all the time. A great way to use up left over Pinto Beans.

½ cup Pinto Beans seasoned with salt only
2 Eggs beaten
1 ½ cups Sugar
1 stick Margarine or Butter melted (1/2 cup)
1 tablespoon Vanilla
½ cup Angel Flake Coconut
1 unbaked Pie Shell

1. Preheat Oven to 350 degrees.
2. Place Pie Shell in pie plate that has been sprayed with cooking spray.
3. Wash Canned Beans and measure ½ cup.
4. Put Beaten Eggs in blender, add Pinto Beans, Sugar, Margarine or Butter and Vanilla. Blend together.
5. Add Coconut and pulse until mixed together.
6. Pour into unbaked pie shell.
7. Bake 40-45 minutes or until brown.

Strawberry Romanoff

2 pints Red Ripe Strawberries
1/3 cup plus 2 tablespoons Sugar
1/3 cup Grand Marnier or Cointreau
Zest from 1 Orange
3/4 cup Heavy Cream

1. Remove stems from Strawberries, rinse well and pat dry with paper towel.
2. Slice Strawberries and place in a bowl.
3. Stir 1/3 cup Sugar and Grand Marnier into Strawberries.
4. Add Orange Zest to Strawberry mixture and place Strawberries in refrigerator until ready to serve.
5. Beat Heavy Cream with 2 tablespoons Sugar and serve over Strawberries.

Sun-Maid Raisin Layer Cake

The Raisin Cake is a favorite of my brother Jim. Momma always made it for him every Christmas. I make it for his birthday every year. This recipe is over 60 years old. Momma found the recipe on a box of Sun-Maid Raisins. It is a very sweet cake with a marshmallow cream icing. You must use plain flour and not cake flour and you must cook the layers completely. Don't make this cake if it is raining since the icing is similar to divinity candy and it will be too sticky if it is humid.

1 ½ cups chopped Raisins - sprinkle 2 tablespoons Flour over
   raisins before adding to batter
3/4 cup Shortening (Crisco)
1 ½ cups Sugar
3 Eggs Separated
2 teaspoons Vanilla
2 1/4 cups All Purpose Flour
3 teaspoons Baking Powder
½ teaspoon Salt
1 cup Milk
3 tablespoons Cocoa
3 tablespoons Hot Milk
½ teaspoon Soda

1. Preheat oven to 350 degrees. Grease and flour 3 - 9 inch cake pans.
2. Put Raisins in hot water for 5 minutes, drain well and chop. Set aside.
3. Using an electric mixer, cream Shortening with Sugar until light and fluffy.
4. Add Egg Yolks and Vanilla to sugar mixture and beat until well mixed.
5. Sift Flour, Baking Powder and Salt and add to batter alternately with Milk.
6. Stir Cocoa into Hot Milk until smooth, add Soda to cocoa mixture and combine with above mixture. Beat just until cocoa mixture is combined with batter.
7. Beat Egg Whites until stiff peaks form and fold Egg Whites into batter using a spatula.
8. Stir in raisins that have been floured.
9. Pour batter into 3 - 9 inch round cake pans.
10. Bake 350 degrees for 20-25 minutes or until a toothpick inserted in

the center comes out clean.

Frosting

1 cup Chopped Raisins
1 cup White Sugar
1 cup Brown Sugar
½ cup Water
3 Egg Whites

1. Put Raisins in hot water for 5 minutes, drain well and chop. Set aside.
2. In a 2 quart saucepan, pour 1/2 cup Hot Water over Sugar. Boil sugar mixture until it spins a thread about 215 degrees using a candy thermometer.
3. Using electric mixer beat Egg Whites until stiff peaks form.
4. Pour syrup over egg whites beating constantly. Beat mixture until cool.
5. Add raisins and beat a little longer.
6. Spread between layers and on top and sides of cake.

Pam's Vegan Raisin Cake

The inspiration for this cake is from a recipe that my Momma found on a Sun-Maid Raisin box. The original icing recipe is made like divinity candy with egg whites. My husband didn't like the original cake because the icing was too sweet for him, but he loves this adaptation. The real test was when I made it for my brother, he couldn't tell the difference from the original.

1 1/2 cups Raisins
3 ¾ cups Whole Wheat Flour plus 3 tablespoons for the
**   Raisins or Freshly Milled Soft White Wheat**
2 teaspoons Baking Powder
2 teaspoons Baking Soda
1 teaspoon Salt
¾ cup Grape Seed Oil
2 cups Sugar
1 cup Non-Dairy Milk
2 teaspoons Vanilla
3 tablespoons Cocoa
3 tablespoons Hot Non-Dairy Milk

1. Grease and flour 2 - 9 inch round cake pans.
2. Preheat Oven to 350 degrees.
3. Put Raisins in bowl with hot water and let sit 10 minutes.
4. Sift Flour three times, the last time add Baking Powder, Baking Soda, and Salt in large bowl. Be sure to put the wheat germ that remains in the sifter back in the flour so you won't lose any of the nutrients.
5. In a separate bowl, wisk Grape Seed Oil, Sugar, Non-Dairy Milk, and Vanilla.
6. Pour wet mixture over dry mixture and wisk together well.
7. Mix Cocoa with Hot Non-Dairy Milk and add to batter, mixing well.
8. Drain Raisins and chop in a food processor. Place raisins in a bowl and dust with 3 tablespoons Flour.
9.   Stir Floured Raisins into batter until well combined.
10. Pour mixture into 2 - 9 inch round cake pans. Bake 25-30 minutes or until a toothpick inserted in center of each pan comes out clean.
11. Cool in pan for 10 minutes then turn out on a wire rack lined with kitchen towel.

12. Cool layers completely before icing.

Icing

1 1/2 cups Raisins
1/2 cup (1 stick) Earth Balance Vegan Buttery Stick softened
8 ounce container Soy Cream Cheese softened
3 cups Vegan Powdered Sugar
1 teaspoon Vanilla
1-2 tablespoons Non-Dairy Milk (if needed)

1. Put Raisins in a bowl with hot water and let sit 10 minutes.
2. Drain Raisins and chop in a food processor, set aside.
3. Using electric mixer, cream Buttery Stick and Soy Cream Cheese.
4. Add Vegan Powdered Sugar and Vanilla and beat until smooth. (Add Non-Dairy Milk if needed).
5. Add Chopped Raisins and beat with mixer until all is combined and icing is fluffy.
6. When cake has cooled, place icing between layers and on top and sides of cake.
7. Cake will keep best in refrigerator between servings.

Rice Pudding

This is not the traditional creamy rice pudding. Momma probably invented it herself since I've never seen a recipe like this. She used left over white rice and baked it in the oven so it is more like a sweet rice casserole.

1 heaping cup White Rice cooked
3/4 cup Sugar
5 ounce can Evaporated Milk mixed with enough Water to make
    1 cup
2 tablespoons melted Butter or Margarine
1 teaspoon Vanilla
1 beaten Egg

1. Preheat oven to 350 degrees and spray an 8 1/2 inch by 4 1/2 inch loaf pan with cooking spray.
2. In a medium size bowl, mix together Rice, Sugar, Milk/Water mixture, Butter, Vanilla and Egg.
3. Pour mixture into prepared pan.
4. Bake 45 minutes.

Jelly, Preserves and Chutney

Apple Chutney

This recipe is from my Aunt Lois, my Daddy's sister. She was a fantastic cook. She put the chutney in the center of canned peaches and baked them. They are so good, it is worth taking the extra time to make this chutney.

1 pound Apples
1/2 pound Tart Apples
1 cup chopped Celery
1 chopped Sweet Red Pepper
1 1/2 cups Vinegar
2 cups Sugar
1 teaspoon Salt
1 cup Seedless Raisins

1. Peel Apples, remove core and chop.
2. Cook Apples and Celery in a small amount of water until tender.
3. While Apples and Celery are cooking, pour hot water over raisins and let sit 20 minutes.
4. Drain Apples and Celery and then to same pan with Apples and Celery add Sweet Red Pepper, Vinegar, Sugar, and Salt. Bring to a rapid boil and cook until clear and slightly thick.
5. Add Raisins and cook 5 minutes.
6. Pour into sterilized jars and seal. Makes about 2 pints.

Peaches with Apple Chutney

1 small can Peach Halves drained
Apple Chutney

1. Preheat oven to 350 degrees.
2. Spray a baking dish that you can fit the Peaches in one layer.
3. Place Peaches in pan and fill center of Peaches with Apple Chutney.
4. Bake about 25 minutes.

Fig Preserves

Daddy always had a fig tree and I still have them in my yard, they must be at least 40 years old now. He loved to make Fig Preserves and since we have the trees and they are abundant in the South, I make them every year. They make great Christmas presents.

2 cups Figs to 1 cup Sugar

*Optional: Slice a Lemon very thin and place entire lemon slices (minus the seeds), rind and all in pan and to cook with figs.

1. Wash and cut Figs into quarters.
2. Pour Sugar over Figs (add Lemon if desired) in heavy pan.
3. Cook until Figs are done, mixture should be slightly brown, syrupy and thick. This will take several hours.
4. Spoon into sterilized jars and put in water bath canner for about 15 minutes. Take jars out of canner and listen for ding to let you know jars have sealed. If you have any jars that did not seal, put in refrigerator.

*Figs have a lot of acid in them so wear plastic gloves when you are washing and cutting them up.

Muscadine or Scuppernong Jelly

Daddy always had some form of grape growing in the yard. He made jelly and wine. Muscadines and Scuppernongs flourish in the South, the Muscadines are purple and the Scuppernongs are green similar to the purple and green grapes from California except they have a tough skin, but the flavor…there is nothing like them.

4 cups Juice
3 cups Sugar

1. To get juice – Wash and crush grapes. Without adding water, boil and simmer for 10 minutes stirring constantly. Press juice from heated grapes. Pour cooled juice into glass container and put in refrigerator overnight. The next day strain the juice.
2. Heat 4 cups juice to boiling in a saucepan.
3. Add 3 cups sugar and stir until sugar dissolves.
4. Boil rapidly over high heat to 8 degrees above the boiling point (220 degrees).
5. Remove pan from heat, skim off foam and put in hot jars.
6. Place jars in water bath canner for 10 minutes. Makes 3 or 4 half pint jars.

Pear Preserves

My Daddy always had a pear tree in the back yard. He made Pear Preserves every summer and they were so delicious with Momma's biscuits. My sister has the knack for making Pear Preserves, hers taste just like Daddy's did.

2 cups Pears to 1 cup Sugar

1. Peel and cut up Pears. (You can cube the pears but I like them better in small long slices.)
2. Pour Sugar over Pears in heavy pan. (If you want chewy preserves, cover and let sit overnight.)
3. Cook until syrup will stand in between fork tines.
4. Spoon into sterilized jars and put in water bath canner for about 15 minutes. Take jars out of canner and listen for ding to let you know jars have sealed. If you have any jars that did not seal, put in refrigerator.

Momma Quotes

He is meaner than a stripped snake.
Don't sit there like a knot on a log.
Sugar wouldn't melt in her mouth.
Hold your horses!
I am worn to a frazzle.
He is a sight for sore eyes.
That is flat as a flitter.
Don't piddle around.
Shake a leg.
She is mad as an old wet hen.
You are going to reap what you sow.
She ain't no spring chicken.
I am plum wore out.
They are like two peas in a pod.
He is still wet behind the ears.
Shut the door, were you raised in a barn?
You are a worry wart.
He is as happy as a dead pig in the sunshine.
I bet that stuck in his craw.
It's comin' up a cloud.
You made your bed, now you have to lay in it.
Don't fly off the handle.
He hollered like a stuck pig.
I do declare.
Now that takes the cake.
He is too big for his britches.
It's as scarce as hen's teeth.
Don't count your chickens before they hatch.
You're going to have to lick your calf over.
Boy, Hidy!
It's as tough as shoe leather.
That is limp as a dishrag.

Howdy do?
There's a whole slew of 'em.
You might ought to.
I am slap wore out.
He had a hissy fit.
Can't never could.

I hope you enjoy making Momma Buttram's Old Fashioned Recipes and sharing them with family and friends as she always did.

My most precious memory and lesson from Momma happened when she was in the hospital a few months before she died. The doctors didn't know what was wrong with her and were running tests. I stayed with her every night and slept on a cot at the foot of her bed. I heard her talking softly and asked what she was saying. She said "I'm praying, I'm thanking God".

Rejoice in the Lord always. I will say it again: Rejoice! Let your gentleness be evident to all. The Lord is near. Do not be anxious about anything, but in every situation, by prayer and petition, with thanksgiving, present your requests to God. And the peace of God, which transcends all understanding, will guard your hearts and your minds in Christ Jesus.

Finally, brothers and sisters, whatever is true, whatever is noble, whatever is right, whatever is pure, whatever is lovely, whatever is admirable—if anything is excellent or praiseworthy—think about such things. Whatever you have learned or received or heard from me, or seen in me—put it into practice. And the God of peace will be with you. Philippians 4:4-9 New International Version Bible

INDEX

Ambrosia, 78

Apple Chutney, 141

Peaches with Apple Chutney, 141

Apple Pie, 79

Apple Pie Hand Held, 80

Baked Apples, Old Fashioned, 81

Baked Apples with Honey, 82

Baked Beans, 35

Baked Ham, 19

Banana Pudding, 83

Barbeque Chicken, 1

Beef Roast, 2

Beef Roast with Onion Gravy, 3

Beef Stew, 4

Biscuits, 71-72

Black Beans, 49

Blueberry Cobbler, 85

Broccoli Casserole, 36

Cabbage, 37

Cake Pan Preparation, 77

Candied Sweet Potatoes, 67

Caramel Cake, 86

Caramel Frosting, 87

Cheese and Macaroni, 40

Cherry Cobbler, 88

Cherry O Cream Cheese Pie, 89

Chicken and Dressing, 7

Chicken and Dumplings, 9

Chicken Brunswick Stew, 10

Chicken Casserole, 5

Chicken Stuffing Casserole, 6

Chocolate Cake Vegan, 92

Chocolate Candy, 94

Chocolate Chip Cookies, 95

Chocolate Fudge Nut Pie, 96

Chocolate Pie, 99

Chocolate Pound Cake, 97

Christmas Cake, 100

Coconut Pie, 102

Cole Slaw, 42

Collards , 38

Collards Vegan, 39

Cooking Dried Beans, 48

Corn Casserole, 43

Cornbread, 73

Country Fried Steak and Gravy, 14

Cream Cheese Pound Cake, 103

Cream Corn, 44

Creamed Beef, 15

Creamed Potatoes, 45

Creole Burgers, 16

Date Nut Roll, 104

Deviled Eggs, 46

Divinity Candy, 105

Dried Beans, 47

English Peas, 50

Fig Preserves, 142

Fried Chicken and Cream Gravy, 11

Fried Irish Potatoes, 58

Fried Okra, 53

Fried Oysters, 26

Fried Pork Chops, 31

Fried Squash, 65

Fruit Cake, 127

Fruit Cake Dark Old Fashioned, 125

Fruit Pie, 108

Fudge Candy, 109

Fudge Pie, 110

Georgia Mud Cake, 90

Goulash, 21

Green Beans, 51

Green Beans Vegan, 52

Ham Soup, 20

Hot Pepper Sauce, 56

Italian Cream Cake, 111

Italian Cream Cake Vegan, 113

Japanese Fruit Cake, 106

Kraut and Wieners, 22

Lane Cake, 115

Lasagna, 18

Lemon Icebox Pie, 119

Lemon Icebox Pie, Baked, 120

Macaroni and Cheese, 41

Maple Pecan Pralines, 122

Mardi Gras Cake, 123

Marinated Vegetable Salad, 68

Meat Balls and Potatoes, 23

Meat Loaf, 24

Mexican Cornbread, 74

Muscadine/Scuppernong Jelly, 143

Okra and Tomatoes, 54

Orange Pecan Pie, 129

Oven Fried Chicken and Cream Gravy, 12

Oyster Stew, 27

Peach Cobbler, 130

Peach Pies Hand Held, 131

Pear Preserves, 144

Pear Salad, 55

Pecan Pie, 132

Pepper Sauce, 57

Pineapple Pudding, 84

Pinto Bean Pie, 133

Pork Chops and Rice, 28

Pork Roast with Sweet Potatoes, 29

Potato Salad served Cold, 61

Potato Salad served Warm, 60

Potatoes in White Sauce, 59

Raisin Cake, 135

Raisin Cake Vegan, 137

Rice Pudding, 139

Rutabaga, 63

Salmon Patties, 32

Scrambled Burger, 17

Spanish Chicken, 13

Spicy Meat Loaf, 25

Squash Casserole, 64

Stewed Squash, 66

Strawberry Pudding, 84

Strawberry Romanoff, 134

Stuffed Pork Chops, 30

Swiss Steak, 33

Turnip Greens, 38

Turnip Greens Vegan, 39

Zucchini Casserole, 69